# The Perfect Match

*by Chris Walkowicz*

HOWELL
BOOK
HOUSE

Wiley Publishing, Inc.

Howell Book House

Published by Wiley Publishing, Inc., New York, NY



For general information on our other products and services or to obtain technical support please contact our Customer Care Department within the U.S. at 800-762-2974, outside the U.S. at 317-572-3993 or fax 317-572-4002.

Wiley also publishes its books in a variety of electronic formats. Some content that appears in print may not be available in electronic books.

Library of Congress Cataloging-in-Publication Data:

Walkowicz, Chris.
The perfect match : a buyer's guide to dogs / by Chris Walkowicz
p. cm.
ISBN 0-87605-767-9
1. Dog Breeds. 2. Dogs—Buying. I. Title
SF426.W36 1996
636.7'1—dc20 96-33471 CIP

Design by Amy Peppler Adams—designLab, Seattle

Manufactured in the United States of America.

20 19 18 17 16 15 14 13 12

# Dedication

*This book is dedicated to all the friends, both canine and human, I've made through the dog world.*

*And to Bonnie Wilcox, DVM, Judie Gulley and Barb Foster, who have suffered through miles and miles of rough drafts.*

# Acknowledgments

*My appreciation to the concerned owners, breeders, club officers and rescuers who cared enough about their breeds to take the time to answer my survey in depth and supply photos. Also to members of the Dog Writers Association of America (DWAA), who are some of the most caring, responsible people in dogs.*

# Contents

# Designer Dogs

Dogs come in more shapes, sizes and colors than Dior designs. Canine designer genes aren't "one size fits all." They have to be customized. No other species offers as many choices. More than 400 breeds were developed for specific purposes; thus, a wide variety of personalities exists. This spectrum of dogs is wonderful, but it's also mind-boggling. How to choose?

In trying to find the ideal dog, first know yourself. Make a list headed "Musts" and "Less important." What can't you tolerate? If your most prized possession is your award-winning flower garden, maybe a perky Pom would be a better choice than a tunneling terrier. Or, if your heart is set on a Cairn, erect a safe, secure pen for your pet's exercise.

The beauty of a long, flowing coat calls for the time and dedication to spend hours brushing, or the finances for professional grooming. Perhaps a patent leather Lab would better suit you.

I enjoy advising puppy seekers about breeds and groups of dogs. But even more important is individual matchmaking. What's great for a family with three teenage boys who like to wrestle and play football is not right for the couple whose favorite pastime is bridge.

During the 30-plus years I've been in dogs, the world has grown more aware of the need for responsible owners and breeders. The primary time dog lovers need to practice responsibility, however, is before succumbing to the seduction of soulful puppy eyes.

A person who is attracted to an Old English Sheepdog for its appealing shagginess and clownish behavior should be aware the attractive coat takes several hours of intensive grooming every week. The owner will also need a perpetual sense of humor or the ability to control a canine clown despite family and career obligations.

The average person cares more about whether Rolff could pull a child on a skateboard and jog with Mom than whether the breed's roots go back to Tibetan Mastiffs and Pekingese. Someone who wants a dog as company for Grandma is more interested in tractability than IQ rating. Shedding is important to the new pet owner; length of neck is not. Eye color is less crucial than possible vision problems.

Understanding the dog's needs and matching them to your own requirements leads to a happy household. Buying a cute puppy on a whim is often the first step on the path to euthanasia. I've been involved in rescue situations where the owner is nice but flustered and exasperated, and the dog is a great but frustrated animal. Together they struck out.

Prospective buyers are learning to ask discerning questions that indicate research before making contact. Yet, few sources offer advice for those looking for a future canine member of the family. This book is to assist buyers in making an informed decision and to aid them in raising a dog responsibly. Dogs that are chosen wisely and raised properly during the first few months are more likely to remain beloved family members. These do not become the sad castaways littering animal shelters and pounds.

Chapter openings describe general characteristics of each group. After studying these, decide whether you would enjoy a dog of the nature described, then search out the breed that most appeals to you. Of course, dogs are individuals and have characteristics that make them the warm, waggly, wonderful creatures they are. I once owned a German Shepherd Dog that was more like a Golden Retriever. But it's best to expect certain tendencies from a dog bred to have those very urges. For instance, you can't really be upset if your Lakeland Terrier stalks your child's hamster or if your Kuvasz creates a ruckus every time a delivery driver knocks at the door.

Once you determine what you desire—or can live with—and what will certainly drive you nuts, you're ready to begin interviewing breeders. In your search, remember you're choosing a breeder as well as a puppy. Find one you can trust, with whom you can build a relationship.

One of the most important rules for the buyer is: Look at the dam, who supplies not only 50 percent of the genetic influence, but all of the environmental influence. If you like the mother, you should like one of her pups. But if there are things that you dislike about her, continue your search for the dog of your dreams.

When buyers learn to look first at the Group, then the breed and, finally, the individuals, understanding their attributes and needs, each pet will be wanted and kept in a nurturing environment for life. Then many shelters, pounds and rescue groups can close their doors.

C.W.

# Alphabetical Listing of Breeds

| | |
|---|---|
| Affenpinscher | Toy |
| Afghan Hound | Hound |
| Airedale Terrier | Terrier |
| Akita | Working |
| Alaskan Malamute | Working |
| American Eskimo Dog | Non-Sporting |
| American Foxhound | Hound |
| American Staffordshire Terrier | Terrier |
| American Water Spaniel | Sporting |
| Anatolian Shepherd Dog | Rare breed |
| Argentine Dogo | Rare breed |
| Australian Cattle Dog | Herding |
| Australian Kelpie | Misc. |
| Australian Shepherd | Herding |
| Australian Terrier | Terrier |
| Basenji | Hound |
| Basset Hound | Hound |
| Beagle | Hound |
| Bearded Collie | Herding |
| Beauceron | Rare breed |
| Bedlington Terrier | Terrier |
| Brussels Griffon | Toy |
| Belgian Malinois | Herding |
| Belgian Sheepdog | Herding |
| Belgian Tervuren | Herding |
| Bernese Mountain Dog | Working |
| Bichon Frise | Non-Sporting |
| Black and Tan Coonhound | Hound |
| Bloodhound | Hound |
| Border Collie | Herding |
| Border Terrier | Terrier |
| Borzoi | Hound |

| | |
|---|---|
| Boston Terrier | Non-Sporting |
| Bouvier des Flandres | Herding |
| Boxer | Working |
| Briard | Herding |
| Brittany | Sporting |
| Bulldog | Non-Sporting |
| Bullmastiff | Working |
| Bull Terrier | Terrier |
| Bull Terrier, Miniature | Terrier |
| Cairn Terrier | Terrier |
| Canaan Dog | Rare breed |
| Cavalier King Charles Spaniel | Toy |
| Chesapeake Bay Retriever | Sporting |
| Chihuahua | Toy |
| Chinese Crested | Toy |
| Chinese Shar Pei | Non-Sporting |
| Chow Chow | Non-Sporting |
| Clumber Spaniel | Sporting |
| Cocker Spaniel (American) | Sporting |
| Collie | Herding |
| Curly-Coated Retriever | Sporting |
| Dachshund | Hound |
| Dalmatian | Non-Sporting |
| Dandie Dinmont Terrier | Terrier |
| Doberman Pinscher | Working |
| Dogue de Bordeaux | Rare breed |
| English Cocker Spaniel | Sporting |
| English Foxhound | Hound |
| English Setter | Sporting |
| English Springer Spaniel | Sporting |
| English Toy Spaniel | Toy |
| Field Spaniel | Sporting |
| Finnish Spitz | Non-Sporting |
| Flat-Coated Retriever | Sporting |
| Fox Terrier | Terrier |
| French Bulldog | Non-Sporting |
| German Pinscher | Rare breed |
| German Shepherd Dog | Herding |
| German Shorthaired Pointer | Sporting |
| German Wirehaired Pointer | Sporting |
| Giant Schnauzer | Working |
| Golden Retriever | Sporting |

| | |
|---|---|
| Gordon Setter | Sporting |
| Great Dane | Working |
| Greater Swiss Mountain Dog | Working |
| Great Pyrenees | Working |
| Greyhound | Hound |
| Harrier | Hound |
| Havanese | Rare breed |
| Ibizan Hound | Hound |
| Irish Red and White Setter | Rare breed |
| Irish Setter | Sporting |
| Irish Terrier | Terrier |
| Irish Water Spaniel | Sporting |
| Irish Wolfhound | Hound |
| Italian Greyhound | Toy |
| Italian Spinoni | Misc. |
| Jack Russell Terrier | Rare breed |
| Japanese Chin | Toy |
| Keeshond | Non-Sporting |
| Kerry Blue Terrier | Terrier |
| Komondor | Working |
| Kuvasz | Working |
| Labrador Retriever | Sporting |
| Lakeland Terrier | Terrier |
| Lhasa Apso | Non-Sporting |
| Lowchen | Rare breed |
| Maltese | Toy |
| Manchester Terrier, Standard | Terrier |
| Manchester Terrier, Toy | Toy |
| Mastiff | Working |
| Miniature Bull Terrier | Terrier |
| Miniature Pinscher | Toy |
| Neapolitan Mastiff | Rare breed |
| Newfoundland | Working |
| Norfolk Terrier | Terrier |
| Norwegian Buhund | Rare breed |
| Norwegian Elkhound | Hound |
| Norwich Terrier | Terrier |
| Old English Sheepdog | Herding |
| Otterhound | Hound |
| Papillon | Toy |
| Pekingese | Toy |
| Petit Basset Griffon Vendéen | Hound |

| | |
|---|---|
| Pharaoh Hound | Hound |
| Plott Hound | Rare breed |
| Pointer | Sporting |
| Polish Owczarek Nizinny | Rare breed |
| Pomeranian | Toy |
| Poodle, Miniature | Non-Sporting |
| Poodle, Standard | Non-Sporting |
| Poodle, Toy | Toy |
| Portuguese Water Dog | Sporting |
| Pug | Toy |
| Puli | Herding |
| Rhodesian Ridgeback | Hound |
| Rottweiler | Working |
| Saint Bernard | Working |
| Saluki | Hound |
| Samoyed | Working |
| Schipperke | Non-Sporting |
| Schnauzer, Giant | Working |
| Schnauzer, Miniature | Terrier |
| Schnauzer, Standard | Working |
| Scottish Deerhound | Hound |
| Scottish Terrier | Terrier |
| Sealyham Terrier | Terrier |
| Shetland Sheepdog | Herding |
| Shiba Inu | Non-Sporting |
| Shih Tzu | Toy |
| Siberian Husky | Working |
| Silky Terrier | Toy |
| Skye Terrier | Terrier |
| Soft-Coated Wheaten Terrier | Terrier |
| Staffordshire Bull Terrier | Terrier |
| Sussex Spaniel | Sporting |
| Tibetan Mastiff | Rare breed |
| Tibetan Spaniel | Non-Sporting |
| Tibetan Terrier | Non-Sporting |
| Treeing Walker Hound | Rare breed |
| Vizsla | Sporting |
| Weimaraner | Sporting |
| Welsh Corgi, Cardigan | Herding |
| Welsh Corgi, Pembroke | Herding |
| Welsh Springer Spaniel | Sporting |
| Welsh Terrier | Terrier |

| | |
|---|---|
| West Highland White Terrier | Terrier |
| Whippet | Hound |
| Wirehaired Pointing Griffon | Sporting |
| Xoloitzcuintli | Rare breed |
| Yorkshire Terrier | Toy |

# 1 Who Says You Can't Buy Love?

*A man was paid to drop a Pit Bull pup with a broken leg into the river in December to drown, but when he changed his mind and sought medical attention, the doctor asked why. He replied, "He was so warm in the hand."*

*John Foote, Allegheny*

## Falling in Love

It's easy to fall in love. And it's not always easy to think clearly when the object of your affection has soft, silky hair and big, warm eyes that plead, "Take me home with you."

So before succumbing to puppy love, quiz yourself. *Do you really want a dog?* What breed is best for you? Adult or puppy? Should you consider adoption or purchase at this particular time?

An animal has specific needs—food, water, exercise, shelter, veterinary care . . . and love. If you can't furnish all these, it's not fair to you or the dog.

Food and water requirements seem simple. A reliable breeder will inform you about amounts and how often to feed that growling tummy. Yet it's not only quantity, but quality that counts. Nutritious food is as important to your dog's well-being as it is to yours. No generics or leftover scraps for this prince of a dog!

Your dog needs regular exercise to stay in good condition, as well as urinate and defecate. If no fenced area is available, an on-leash walk is necessary several times a day, as is a leg-stretching romp in a safe area or on a flexible leash at least once a week.

Adequate shelter is necessary for protection from the elements. Your dog will want private moments just as people do, and will seek a protected place for sleeping. Animals in the wild seek a cave or den; a modern dog is content with an individual house, bed or crate.

Even a healthy dog needs regular inoculations and examinations to help prevent serious disease. A responsible owner provides preventive as well as emergency and regular veterinary care.

*Puppy love*

Sad rescue situations show that animals, like people, can live without some of these necessities for a short period of time. But they do not thrive. Dogs always want your attention, approval and assurance.

It's not a good idea to buy a pet for a child or anyone else in the family unless you like dogs, too. You also have to live with the animal, and chances are you'll be responsible for the care at times. The parent who grudgingly buys a dog to teach a child responsibility is in for a shock. Parents who believe Melissa when she promises she will take care of the pup need to be prepared for reality. What about the remote-controlled car you gave Junior last Christmas? Is he still enjoying it as he did in the beginning? Is the doll Melissa begged for now headless in the sandbox? Should children not live up to their part of the bargain or a spouse take a new job with extended traveling, you can't just cancel a subscription. Like the introductory quote from Allegheny, dogs are "so warm in the hand." You can't stick them in the back of the closet like a pair of outgrown jeans; they still need love and care. *Your dog is going to be around for a number of years.*

*Your dog needs exercise.*

Thought beforehand saves pain later for everyone. Sometimes the answer is not a dog at all. Maybe it's a cat . . . or a *stuffed animal.*

Dogs are always there when you need them. No matter if a child can't leave the house, she always has a friend. If you lose your job, your pup won't yell at you. If your children fail a test, their dog still looks up to them.

*But,* is this the right time to have a dog? Even lifelong dog lovers should face the fact that their circumstances might have changed in regard to finances, living quarters or leisure time. Perhaps we can still manage a dog, but we should bear these changes in mind. A smaller or less energetic breed might do, or maybe we should skip over the adorable but demanding puppy and consider an adult.

An older dog is usually housebroken, is done teething and is able to stay alone for longer periods of time. Breeders occasionally have an older puppy or dog that didn't turn out to be the show star they'd hoped for, or that just needs a one-dog home. Sometimes an adult is available to a suitable home to enjoy years in blissful retirement. This might be a Champion, Obedience titled dog or former brood matron; often this gem is trained. Many fanciers also participate in purebred rescue, saving dogs from sure death or lives of misery. Now and then breeders know of a dog available due to an owner's death or change of circumstances.

*Dogs are love money can buy.* Even the one given to you by a puppy-laden neighbor costs money. The free dog is not always the most reasonable. No matter what the initial purchase price, a medium-sized (about forty pounds) dog costs about $500—or more—a year to maintain:

- About $150 of quality dog food.
- Dog licenses run from $5.
- Basic vet care costs at least $150 for exams, vaccinations, flea control and heartworm prevention.
- Of course, a larger dog eats more food and requires a larger dose of heartworm preventative.
- If professional grooming is needed, add another $150-plus per year.
- To begin with, you'll need to buy supplies such as a collar, leash, bowls and housing.
- Other smart investments include a training class and fencing the yard or an exercise area.

Prices for purebred pups vary, depending on the breed. Most people, when considering their first purchase of a dog, are interested only in a pet and companion. A show prospect may be more expensive.

For people who are afraid of dogs, owning one will change their view forever. But it's best to make friends with someone else's dog first, rather than buying a cuddly pup on impulse. Walk a friend's dog, offer to dogsit for a weekend, or exercise and water your neighbor's new pup while she's at work. Most people find their fear was caused by a particular dog, not all canines.

When you've considered all these things and have decided the time and expense are worth the companionship and devotion, let yourself go. Fall in love!

## The Match Game

So you've made the decision. You want to share your life with a dog—but what breed? The 400 breeds registered by the American Kennel Club (AKC), United Kennel Club (UKC), Federation Cynologique Internationale (FCI) and kennel clubs throughout the world offer something for every dog lover.

Registration papers are issued for dogs with registered parents and certified by the breeder to be purebred. *These papers are not a guarantee of quality*, nor a Good Housekeeping seal of approval. Dogs are only as good as their breeder.

Most potential dog owners have some idea of what type appeals to them: large or small, hairy or smooth, active or quiet. All that's left is to narrow down the choices. The various attributes of the breeds, plus individual personalities, allow everyone to obtain the perfect match.

Which breed to choose?

## Sorting Them Out

Certain breeds are often groomed professionally and some must be brushed frequently. Others come with wash-and-wear coats. A long-haired dog is gorgeous when combed and gleaming. But the same animal looks filthy and tangled if the owner doesn't brush and care for the coat.

Everything sheds! Nothing dies with the same hair it is born with. Contrary to popular opinion, *long hair does not shed more than short*—it just has more length! Longer hair often makes *less* mess around the house, the clumps being easier to pick up than zillions of little pointy hairs sticking in cushions or carpet. Proper and consistent grooming usually removes dead hair. Even those who suffer allergies or prefer to avoid dog fluff wafting about the house can find happiness with hairless breeds or those that shed minimally.

Although a large dog can take up a lot of room in a small apartment, a lethargic giant uses less space than a tiny dynamo dashing from sofa to window to front door back to sofa. Most dogs are content in their owner's home, be it huge or humble. One of the big breeds can do just as well in the city as the country, as long as the animal receives the proper exercise. The amount of activity a dog requires does not depend on size alone, but on attitude. Some of the giant breeds, for instance, are happiest when snoozing in the sun. High-energy breeds demand daily vigorous exercise. Frisky dogs are more in tune with a jogging family than an eighty-year-old needlepoint devotee.

Tiny breeds are *not* the best choice for a family with small tots. Big dogs have a reputation for being easygoing and patient with children. A giant breed is not as likely to be injured by a slamming door or a toddler. The dog might rise, knocking down the infant on a well-cushioned bottom, but doesn't need to retaliate with teeth.

Conversely, choice is not limited to large breeds if you are looking for a dog to protect your family and property. Statistics show that persons, homes and businesses with doggie doorbells are avoided as victims of break-ins and attacks. Dwarf or giant, dogs make a lot of noise—yaps, growls and booming barks serve as canine alarm systems. It is simpler for the intruder to go on to the next place. Besides, little teeth hurt as much as big ones.

A member of the larger breeds can be more difficult to manage because of mass and weight. It is harder to nudge a Saint Bernard over the car seat than even the most defiant Toy breed!

A few dogs prefer one or two persons and remain aloof from others. Some breeds love playing and tumbling on the floor with children. Let's face it; kids are noisy, enthusiastic creatures. They shriek. They run. They slam doors. This can make even devoted parents' nerves stand up and quiver. Excitable dogs can be driven to distraction; calm, placid breeds join the fun or snore through the commotion.

A good relationship is difficult to develop when you're separated from the rest of the family. Bonding is easy when your pet is your shadow by day and your footwarmer at night. But it's convenient to ignore the urge to scratch behind an ear when you have to go to the backyard to do it. More likely your only contact will be to holler at the dog to shut up when the lonely howling begins. Nevertheless, some circumstances demand an outdoor domicile for the canine member of the family. A few breeds must live indoors and suffer from extremes in temperatures. Others adapt to any weather with adequate shelter. But all dogs do better when inside with the family at least part of every day.

A houseful of precious objects calls for a graceful, mannerly dog. Rough-and-tumblers suit a family with a casual lifestyle.

Whatever your hobby—whether it's hunting, biking or sledding—there's a dog panting to join the fun. Some dogs look elegant lying in front of a fireplace or on a satin pillow. A few bristle at your best friend; others greet any and all effusively.

If you want a purebred, registered dog, attend a dog show. For an overview of all AKC breeds, watch the Westminster Kennel Club show, telecast annually in February. Shows offer classes for most of the breeds in this book. Magazines and local clubs can furnish information on dates and sites of shows. Plan a full day to observe several breeds. Catalogs giving owner information and time schedules for each breed are available. Study behavior and personality of the breeds you are considering, both in and out of the rings. When exhibitors are finished showing, they are willing to talk about their dogs and answer your questions. Be prepared for a rosy picture, as all fanciers are enchanted with their chosen breed. If you really wish to know whether a particular breed sheds or can run a marathon, ask. Breeders want their puppies to be happy, and the best way to ensure this is for the new owners to be happy too.

When you've settled on one or two breeds, *read* everything you can find on them (especially breed books) to obtain various authorities' viewpoints. Concentrate on the chapters covering character to see whether this is really the dog for you. Seek out examples so you can view them in the flesh and interact with them.

## Where Can I Find My Best-Friend-to-Be?

Dogs are easy to find, but make the extra effort to find the *right* one. Dogs may be found at pounds, humane societies, via newspaper ads, at shows, in pet shops, through friends, clubs or magazines—even on street corners. The Internet can make connections, particularly for hard-to-find breeds.

If you open your heart and home to a stray, whether purebred or a mix, you are doing a good deed. It's a lifesaver for the dog, which would likely be a pound statistic or road kill otherwise. Adopting a foundling is also a good deed for society, as this dog won't chase and destroy farm stock. This particular animal will then not bite-and-run, dirty the streets, strew garbage or create more homeless canines.

Whether the story has a happy ending for you, however, only time will tell. When environmental circumstances and genetic influences molding your dog's temperament are unknown, you're groping in the dark, unable to see what's ahead. If this is what your heart tells you to do and you're prepared to face and conquer problems, bless you. But if you only think this is an inexpensive way to obtain a pet, it does neither you nor the dog any good to rerun this scenario.

Animal control officers pick up strays or temporarily house the unwanted pets that are unloaded at their door like yesterday's newspaper. Animals are shifted through pounds within a short period. The time limit is but a few days, and when it's up, they are destroyed. Again, the background of these dogs is uncertain.

Pounds are a nightmare to the soft-hearted and to the officials who must decide which live or die. Be prepared to harden your resolve, or you'll walk out accompanied by every dog in the cages. Keep in mind what you want from your future companion, and think with your mind as well as your heart. The most appealing dog could be the worst one for you to live with.

Humane societies do their best for as long as they can with available funds. Dogs are examined and treated if not badly diseased or injured. Animals with the best chance at adoption are kept the longest. This means healthy, attractive, friendly dogs. Puppies have a better chance than adults. Small dogs are easier to place than large ones. Many people start out preferring purebreds, and shaggy, furry ones have a better placement ratio than their smooth-coated counterparts.

Some charities keep the animals until they are adopted, creating their own set of problems. A few animals live their entire lives in a cage or kennel run. These dogs become canine autistics, ritually spinning or pacing, unable to interact. Without the human bonding dogs crave, they face life in doggie prison. When the shelters are full, the homeless must seek shelter elsewhere, and still face death row.

All these organizations have an adoption fee, a portion of which may be refundable following the required neutering of the pet. Expense is minimal for the person adopting. The cost to the animal's mental and physical stability, however, is sometimes too great.

Try to determine a background by asking questions concerning the dog's life, at least during the shelter stay. If the dog is a purebred German Shepherd Dog or a Beagle mix, read appropriate breed literature, books, pamphlets or articles before you decide whether this is the perfect match for you. Ask the workers:

- Is there any genetic history? (Owners of the surrendered dog may have left information. Strays have no known history, so be prepared for anything.)
- Have any behavioral or physical problems been noted? (If the dog has been turned in for a specific problem or one has been demonstrated at the shelter, can you deal with this or solve it?)
- Are there medical records? (Is there a physical problem that will be costly? Do you care if the dog's ear is missing?)

For the survivors, rescue is a lifesaver. Purebred rescue groups provide foster homes until the dogs are ready for a new home. During this time, temperament is assessed. Only sound dogs that can be rehabilitated are offered for adoption. All are neutered and given a veterinary examination with proper treatment. Some of the rarer breeds have waiting lists for rescues. Most ask for a donation to cover at least expenses so efforts can continue.

Pet shops might display an adorable "doggie in the window," and before the unprepared public realizes, they're in the shop asking, "How much?" Stores do not breed these animals themselves. The dogs come from people who have not been able to sell them or who breed only to make a living by having a product to sell. The pups may be rejects, or they may be the results of "puppy mill" operations that raise dogs as a cash crop. These people indiscriminately breed in volume and sell the pitiful results at the earliest possible age to a broker. While the shops themselves might be clean, the medical attention the pup received prior to reaching the facility is unknown. The proprietors are not familiar with the ancestors or whether the pedigree (if there is one) is accurate. Sales clerks, and probably the puppy mill owners, won't know whether the pup's parents suffer hereditary defects and aren't aware of breed predispositions or specific characteristics.

The retailer is the end of a mass production line. After the breeder and middlemen have been paid, the price at a pet shop is often higher than a direct purchase from a breeder.

Some pet supply stores now direct their efforts toward arranging adoptions from local humane societies. They display animals, helping to groom, socialize and care for them. If you decide to purchase a dog through a retail store, determine whether it comes from a lifesaving shelter or from a so-called "breeder." *Remember, strictly speaking, a breeder is only the person who owns or leases a bitch that has puppies.* That means that every puppy has a breeder, but not everyone who breeds a litter is conscientious.

Owners who allow—or arrange for—Flossie to have an occasional litter are termed "backyard breeders." They're only having puppies because they want Princess to have a litter before they spay her or before she's too old. Maybe all their neighbors and friends think Dusty is a terrific dog and *say* they would like to have one just like her. Or maybe Duchess herself made the decision to become a mother. Most people who allow their dogs to be bred indiscriminately, however, are not conscientious about genetic testing. They have no idea what the difference is between congenital (present from birth) and genetic (inheritable) defects. If the litter is purebred, they might ask a low price. Registered pups are usually more. If the litter is Duchess' choice rather than theirs, and the father was a drifter, the owners will be fortunate to receive five dollars. These people "get rid" of the pups as early as possible to keep expenses to a minimum. Puppies are expensive to raise, as well as a lot of work, and the more they grow, the more they eat and demand in care.

Conscientious, responsible breeders raise puppies only when they have several advance reservations. They have the experience of years in owning and studying their chosen breed(s). The dam of the litter is valuable, not only in sentimental or financial worth, but as the result of careful, selective breeding. Only the perfect stud will do. Good breeders spare no expense for the mating, sometimes choosing a mate thousands of miles away, and the puppies and dam are treated like royalty. The dogs receive premium food, the best medical care and all the attention they deserve. These breeders realize that if they skimp anywhere, the puppies suffer, and so does their reputation. Soundness cannot be built on cutting corners.

When searching for a reputable breeder, call local kennel clubs for suggestions. AKC has a 900 number with breed information (1-900-407-PUPS). Talk to a veterinarian. Look objectively (if you can) at several litters. It doesn't matter where you finally obtain your dog as long as the choice is the one most compatible with you.

No matter where you find your pup, insist on registration papers, complete medical records and proof that genetic testing has been done on the parents. Make an appointment with a veterinarian immediately for a complete exam and necessary inoculations.

## It Pays to Be Choosy

Okay, you've decided. It's got to be a "Schnocklefritz." It likes kids, is medium-sized and intelligent. It's active, short-haired and friendly. You may have already met a Schnocklefritz breeder at one of the shows you've attended. Assuming you like the dogs from that kennel, they might have puppies due and can take your reservation. If they are not planning a litter, they should be able to refer you to another responsible breeder. Clubs often have referral lists. Several dog magazines showcase advertisements from breeders.

Call the breeder for an appointment, stating your wishes. Write a note outlining important and preferred characteristics. This gives the breeder something to refer to when evaluating and matching pups with owners.

Be prompt for your appointment. Breeders have busy lives. They might have postponed departure for a show to meet you. They could have six Schnocklefritzen to groom, a mating to handle and another prospective buyer eagerly waiting. If you can't be on time or need to cancel, make a courtesy call. It is upsetting to bathe three puppies and have no one show up at the party!

Ask to see the pedigree of the pup. A pedigree is a written lineage, a "family tree." Obviously, even poorly bred dogs and mixed breeds have ancestors. It's not having a pedigree that counts—it's what's in the pedigree. Even if you don't know what you're looking for in a pedigree, a dedicated breeder has one ready to show you and can describe the dogs therein and explain various titles. Although you may not be interested in showing, titles indicate intelligence, good temperament and sound bodies of ancestors—things we all want.

Taking into consideration the fact that brood matrons are not at their glamorous best, you should like the dam's looks. Breeders rarely own the sire, sometimes traveling great distances for a mating. Ask to see a picture of the sire if you can't see him in the flesh. The breeder should have verification of sound hips and avoidance of any other hereditary problems that commonly occur in Schnocklefritzen. You should like the mother enough to want to take her home because, in a sense, you will be. Puppies often mimic the mother in temperament. Is she alert, proud, sweet, protective, timid or whatever you prefer?

Puppies are always adorable, no matter what the breed. It's easy to fall for one immediately, but be patient. Ask questions. Explain why you decided on a Schnocklefritz. Discuss whether you plan to breed, field trial or show in either conformation or obedience. Breeders will be able to point out which pups are showing positive or negative tendencies for these careers. I encourage my buyers to keep their minds open as to gender, instead choosing the personality that suits them.

People aren't perfect, and neither are puppies. One might have an improper bite or incorrect ear set. Another could be an undesirable color, have an incorrect coat or, in males, an undescended testicle—all common faults that allow you, the future owner, to have a wonderful pet even if the puppy is not a show prospect. If one of these imperfections turns you off, admit it. *A conscientious breeder requires these puppies to be neutered, and/or sells them with limited AKC registration, so that their offspring cannot be registered.*

Medical records should include an exam, fecal check for parasites, deworming if necessary and at least one combination vaccination. Because the dam passes her immunity and innate health to the pups, she should be robust and have current immunization. Sound parents increase the chances of sound progeny.

Inquire about a health guarantee. Obtain a written contract that covers for a minimum of one year any serious defect for which the breeder could be responsible. In addition, you should be assured a full refund within 48 hours should the pup not pass a veterinary exam because of a serious problem. Of course, the breeder cannot promise the pup will never have any problems, any more than an adoption agency could. But ethical breeders stand behind their pups and offer a partial refund or replacement if your pet has a congenital disorder, which will seriously alter either the dog's life or yours. Don't be swept away by sweet puppy kisses if there is no health guarantee.

Beware the listless or shy pup hiding from attention. Do not pick a pitiful pup because you feel sorry for it. If you do, you could feel sympathy pangs for another ten or fifteen years. Watch the interaction of each individual with other puppies and the breeder as well as with you. But remember, a dedicated breeder's observation during the pup's eight weeks of life is probably more accurate than your eight-minute viewing.

When breeders have given you their suggestions, ask whether they've done temperament tests. These are one more way of confirming your own and breeders' observations. It's important to remember this is a test in which no one passes or fails. One pup might be better suited to the elderly couple—or the former Marine drill sergeant.

*Evaluate movement and other qualities.*

, puppies should be eight weeks or older when moving to their new home. By then, they're weaned, vaccinated and ready to face challenges. If you're choosing a show prospect, it should be old enough for evaluation of movement and other qualities.

Ask for a reading list on the breed and information on training. A demonstration of grooming, nail trimming and ear cleaning and plucking, if necessary, is helpful. Breeders can inform you of the address of the national club for that breed and might be able to suggest a local club or classes. If you have questions that arise later, contact the breeder. Most are happy to hear of their puppies' progress and to help if they can.

Remember, you're choosing a breeder as well as a puppy. Find a knowledgeable person you can trust and who will be available to support you during the puddles of housebreaking, the worry of illness, the frustration of yellow ribbons rather than blue and, eventually, the grief of loss.

Prepare a list of questions such as the following to ask the breeder:

- How many years have you bred dogs? This breed?
- How many litters do you breed a year? (More is NOT better.)
- For which traits do you breed?
- What faults do you see in your own dogs?
- Can I see the dam?
- Are the dam and sire x-rayed and certified free of hip dysplasia?
- Are the parents free of any serious hereditary disorders?
- What problems does this breed have? (Don't believe anyone who says "None.")
- What drawbacks does this breed have? (Ditto!)
- Have you shown your dogs? Do they have titles?
- Do you belong to Breed Specialty or all-breed clubs? (These can serve as breeder references.)
- Do you temperament test?
- Can I see the pedigree and contract?
- Can I see the medical history of the litter?
- Do you offer a guarantee?
- What is the life expectancy of the breed? What's the oldest dog you've owned?

*Your dog's den*

At the same time, notice the surroundings of the kennel:

- Note whether the premises and dogs are clean.
- Knickknacks and breed paraphernalia show a long-term commitment to the breed and a love that goes beyond the price of the pup.
- Make sure the dam has the kind of temperament and personality you desire in your pup.
- Are the dogs happy?
- Do the dogs seem healthy?
- Look for loving interaction between owner and dogs.
- Does the breeder seem knowledgeable?
- Does the breeder seem enthusiastic about the breed?
- Would I like to have a long-term relationship with this person?

In addition, a conscientious breeder will cover various concerns:

- Why you want a dog and how you chose this breed
- Whether you have proper facilities
- How you intend to confine the dog—fence, pen, crate, walking on leash
- Feeding instructions
- The expense of pet ownership
- Grooming requirements
- Suggestions for training
- Neutering requirements or, alternatively, show and health demands prior to breeding
- Pet ownership as a long-term commitment
- Whether you've owned other dogs and what happened to them

During your visit, the breeder will be watching you with the dogs and their response to you. Your conversation will end with an invitation (or demand!) to keep in touch and a command to call if, for any reason, you cannot keep the dog.

Your pup might not be perfect. But, if you do your homework, you'll think he is!

## What Is a Pet?

To dog lovers, the word "pet" is synonymous with "dog." To a dog fancier, "pet" has a different meaning. Breeders hope and desire that each pup, including that famed "pick of the litter," will be someone's beloved companion. We want the buyer to love that puppy the way we have.

Pets have the same number of legs as show dogs, the same number of bones, a noisemaker located just under the nose, a fast-licking tongue and hair that sheds. So what's the big deal?

Show puppies are the best prospects for finishing Championships. A showable pup is promising, but not as outstanding. Each breed has its own Standard, depicting the ideal. The Standards list faults and attributes. Since a perfect dog has yet to be born, even show dogs possess minor faults. Some Standards note disqualifications. These dogs cannot be shown in conformation. The AKC regulations state that retained testicles are a disqualification in all breeds.

Size, color and coat length are of little significance to the pet owner. Other disqualifications or faults include poor coat texture, improper eye color and faulty tail carriage or ear set. All of these less-than-perfect dogs can be good pets, as long as they have the most important qualities: health and temperament. An over-, under- or wry bite is not life-threatening. Pet owners are more concerned about "will he or won't he" bite than whether his teeth are straight.

Bilateral cryptorchidism means that neither testicle descended. The common term "monorchidism" is often used for one retained. Because dogs that fail to meet the breed Standard should be neutered, a cryptorchid will be no different from any other pet after the surgery.

Lack of attitude simply means the dog does not have enough sparkle to win in the ring. Actually, those dogs that lack the extra zip and animation for life on the show circuit are sometimes easier for the average person to live with.

High-set ears or ones that don't stand or fold properly may zap a show career, but a lop-eared dog can still hear a chewbone drop a mile away or a voice inviting her for a romp. At the other end, tails may be low-set or carried too gaily over the back, but they still wag the same when you walk in the door.

Undersized or oversized for the show ring may actually be ideal for the pet owner. Sizes listed for each breed are preferred. Individual pets can have a greater range.

The rarity of show dogs is the reason they are more valuable financially. The reality is that the largest percentage of a litter goes to pet homes.

A caring breeder treats all pups equally. They receive the same food, medical attention and socialization. In most instances, no one can tell positively which pup is show and which is pet until the litter is several weeks old. Besides, good breeders love all dogs and would never neglect any pup.

*The differences between a show dog and a pet may not be obvious to the untrained eye.* Examples are infinitesimal flaws in movement, angulation or extension of gait. Without a period of intense study, most observers will never know. And you'll still think you have the greatest dog on earth.

Although these and other points may matter a great deal to the professional, they won't mean a whit to the person just looking for a good friend. After all, we don't judge our human friends by the length of their hair, their overbite or how fast they can run the mile. So a pet's not perfect, just like us. But most importantly, a pet is a dog God made for love.

## Purebred or All-American?

Every dog needs a home, and the mixed-breed dog is no exception. When Champion Muppet next door is caught unaware by Casanova from the corner, your neighbor might become very friendly.

A family's decision to welcome a dog to their hearth must be determined by mind over heart. All things considered, do you want a dog? If so, do you want Muppet's offspring? If the answer's no, put a fence around your property and buy Junior a softball.

Crossbreeds can be good pets. Your "pomador" could be the best dog you ever own. The only trouble is you're less likely to be able to predict what that dog will look or act like. Even when both parents of a mixed litter are known, it is difficult to guess what pups will look like or how they'll behave. It's impossible to know how large the pups will be as adults.

Frequently, with an unplanned litter of the mother's choice, the sire is unknown by anyone—except the mother and she's not talking. *Congenital defects, or worse yet, hidden illnesses that surface at a later time are not restricted to purebred dogs.* Mixed breeds and purebreds alike can be healthy or sickly. They can also be shy or friendly, strong or weak, smart or dull, cute or homely, small or big, tough or timid, bouncy or lazy, quiet or noisy. *The difference is that purebred breeders know what to expect.*

Breeders are often aware of a problem within their lines and might be prepared to cull the litter by placing with neutering contracts or by euthanasia if necessary. If a defect comes to surface in an older dog, good breeders are prepared to contend with the difficulty.

Some attributes show up at birth. Color is often apparent, although with some breeds, color can fade or darken. Birth defects such as cleft palate or hydrocephalus can be determined quickly. Many traits commonly become distinct about the age of two to three months, but it is customary for owners of a nondescript litter to wean the hungry little yappers early and place them immediately at the age of five weeks.

Sadly, the more valuable a possession, the better the care. Most owners who have to give away pups don't want to invest money in veterinary care. The recipient of the pup must be prepared for the extra expense. Sometimes post-purchase health care amounts to as much as the price of a purebred pup.

If owners are happy with the results, the relationship can be good. Because genetic background is unknown, a serious or even fatal disorder such as dilated esophagus or heart valve defect may become apparent just as the pup has endeared itself to family members.

Temperament is an iffy matter with accidental breedings. These dogs often lack the socialization necessary with people and siblings because of early departure from the nest. Maybe the dam has good temperament, but there is no way of knowing whether the sire is a kiss-and-run sweetheart—or a love 'em and leave 'em nasty guy. When very different types of dogs breed, such as a Pomeranian and Labrador mix, you have no idea whether the results will be an eighty-pound lap dog or an eight-pound retriever. The lofty misnomer of "schnoodle" or "cockapoo" or "pekapoo" does not mean your dog will be as predictable as the Schnauzer dam or Poodle sire. When two (or more) breeds are mixed, the purity of both breeds is lost. The "pekapoo" you hoped would not shed much might do just that. The "pekcock" you expected to be merry may not be, even if your last one was. You cannot expect a mix to run true to form.

*No one keeps statistics on mixed breeds, and there are no specific studies for researching their disorders.* But all dogs—and their owners—benefit from health studies conducted and funded by Parent Clubs and dedicated fanciers.

No matter what the breed or blend of breeds, they all need care and love. Taking the care to find the right one for you means happiness for yourself and your pet. Whatever the breed or multi-breed of your choice, rare, unusual or popular, somewhere there is a dog that will fit you perfectly.

# 2

# Reading Between the Lines, or *Caveat Emptor*

This book was written by interviewing hundreds of experienced owners—people who care deeply about their puppies, their breed and dogs in general. They gave their time, hoping that with knowledgeable purchase the need for rescue would be lower. Their advice is golden. If everyone *buying or breeding* a dog would strive to become responsible, rescue societies could turn to raising funds for veterinary research, holding educational seminars or going home to shower affection on their own dogs.

A common thread appeared through nearly every survey. Breeders are just as concerned (or perhaps more so) in finding good buyers as the reverse.

Many needs are not breed specific. Thus some universal rules are in order.

**Choose your dog wisely**

First, choose a breed that is age appropriate. Several breeds issue a warning concerning small children. This includes infants who will become toddlers, couples who will someday have children, and grandparents or others who have little visitors.

In some instances, particularly with Toy breeds, awkward or well-meaning toddlers could injure the dog by dropping, holding too tight or falling on the animal. In other cases, it's the child's safety at stake. Extremely large or boisterous dogs could knock over a tot. Small dogs might snap if they can't escape. Herding dogs sometimes nip at heels or buttocks. Guardian breeds, while often tolerant—if not loving—of their own charges, can object to raucous visitors running in and out, the shouting and screeching of excited children and the pushing and shoving that goes on in play. Occasionally, these dogs will protest even a parental correction.

All of this doesn't mean you can't have your Perfect Match. Wait until the children are older. Use common sense. Supervise play. Instruct kids in how to respect their pet and teach the dog to be gentle. Confine the dog when play reaches sonic boom level or the animal becomes overexcited.

*The perfect match?*

A reminder here of one of the most important pieces of advice: Look at the dam. Does she accept your children? Is she gentle? Are the kids intimidated? *Are they kind to the dog?*

Slight variations will occur in even the best-bred litters. Choose an outgoing, confident (but not rowdy) pup.

### Ask about health, but don't panic

Problems listed range from occasional to common occurrence within the breed. Individual lines differ. Health clearances in most instances are for the parents. A few tests, such as heart and juvenile cataract exams, are performed on puppies. Consult with a veterinarian about which tests are pertinent for puppies in your chosen breed.

Conditions listed are only those that could alter the lives of the dog and the owner, i.e., life-threatening, crippling, painful or those that are expensive or time-consuming to treat. The most frequent problems mentioned were skin and flea allergies. Because this can occur in any dog and is annoying but not dangerous, this was not included.

Anesthesia sensitivity is common with sighthounds and short-muzzle (brachycephalic) dogs. Breeds with the highest incidence of hip dysplasia (more than 20 percent per OFA) are listed with an asterisk following the notation HD.

Disorders that are obvious and/or fatal before selling age of eight weeks (i.e., dwarfism, hydrocephalus or spina bifida) are not noted. For these and other defects that would have a deleterious effect on dogs owned by people intending to breed or exhibit, ask your vet and see *Successful Dog Breeding,* by Chris Walkowicz and Bonnie Wilcox, DVM (Howell Book House).

Continue the breeder's initial care by scheduling physicals as needed. Remember to make the first veterinary appointment soon after picking up your pup.

### Confine your dog

A fenced yard is preferred by most sellers. All dogs, even lazy ones, need exercise. Humans, being human, find it difficult to brave a sub-zero trot to the nearest fire hydrant. It's more convenient to open the back door at 2 A.M. than to blearily don coat and shoes to walk a puppy answering a sudden call of nature. And it's sometimes hard to find time for a walk on the night you have to rush home from work, prepare dinner and leave for the kids' ballgame or dance recital. Fences do more than provide a space for exercise. They're safety precautions, keeping Bowser in and others out. They protect tiny dogs from being injured, those with the wanderlust from being lost or hit by a car, and the overprotective from causing a lawsuit.

City dwellers can provide wonderful, loving homes as well. Walks on leash are an acceptable substitute.

### Shelter your dog

All dogs, from the teeniest to the BIGGEST, need shelter. With adequate exercise and training, plus finding the Perfect Match for your lifestyle, any dog can make a good house pet. Kennel dogs must have protective housing.

Breeders, almost without exception, voted for inside living conditions. Even the breeds that tolerated high and low temperatures and could survive outside were deemed to thrive only if inside, or at least with quality time spent with their owners.

## Groom your dog

Basic grooming needs are not breed-specific and were not included in the individual listings. Every dog needs nails clipped, ears cleaned, teeth brushed and bathing. Depending on certain aspects such as length of hair or attraction to dirt and foul smells, pets are bathed as needed—between monthly and biannually. Nails usually have to be trimmed every three to four weeks. Ears should be cleaned at the same time unless the breed is one that requires more frequent attention. Most owners brush the dog's teeth during the weekly session, but some do it as often as every day. Dental exams should be scheduled as needed.

Despite boasts to the contrary, *all dogs shed*—except hairless ones. Long-haired breeds shed in clumps; short-haired ones lose one hair at a time, which can stick to furniture and clothing. When some dogs lose hair, it doesn't fall on the floor but becomes twisted within the existing coat. These dogs require grooming to avoid mats and sores, as well as to look neat.

Many allergic buyers believe the hair, or the length of it, can be problematic. Rather, the skin dander is the allergen. Long hair can carry more pollen or other symptom-causing substances. Keeping the dog ultra-clean helps, as does having the pet sleep elsewhere than the bedroom.

## Train your dog

All dogs benefit from the socialization, bonding and leadership definition gained from attending a puppy kindergarten and an obedience class, as well as practicing at home. Owners receive benefits too: a well-behaved dog with good house manners, one that greets visitors calmly and happily while not ripping stockings or snarling in their faces. Training makes timid dogs more courageous and obnoxious ones more controllable. Dominant dogs accept a lower place in the chain of command.

One caveat: No harsh handling. Little dogs can be hurt, timid ones become more frightened, dominant dogs dig in their heels, aggressive ones fight back. The consequence is the same. The dogs simply won't do it, and problems escalate.

All owners remarked about the intelligence of their breed choice. This is true! When fulfilling an inborn urge, there is none better. Take your dog's instincts into consideration when teaching house manners and take advantage of this innate intelligence.

With rare exceptions (those from the three or four top Obedience breeds), all breeders noted that their dogs became bored with repetition. Although it may be difficult to find a nearby class where the trainer makes things fun and interesting, the owner can innovate at home.

After the basics are mastered, go to a park, or near a schoolyard or a shopping center and try the following:

- With the dog at Heel, break into a fast trot from a standstill.
- Halt in the middle of a sprint.
- When your dog starts to look away, turn suddenly.
- Utilize more than the sidewalk.
- Climb a dirt mound, halting once halfway up and again going down.
- Walk at the side of the road for a few feet.
- Go up and down gullies or around a trash can.

Make training so doggoned interesting, your pet's eyes follow you everywhere and dance with excitement when you bring out the leash. "Proof" the dog with distractions—a cat, a kid on a bike, a lawnmower across the street. Have a beloved person leave in the car without him. When a dog obeys in the middle of a three-ring circus, that's dependability!

It's important. Obedience may save the dog's life and will certainly save your sanity.

**Take charge of your dog**

Dogs originally lived in packs. Even today, when they're born, they're part of a litter and raised with the pack. In every group, there must be a leader. To keep the

*Dogs are pack animals.*

peace, everyone else is a follower. Just as parents guide children to keep them safe and to become good citizens, so owners must guide pets.

Calm, consistent, confident instructions will teach the dog that YOU are the leader. The dog, no matter how cute, no matter how treasured, must remain at the bottom of the pecking order. Or this little cuddly pup will grow up to be a spoiled brat, one with sharp teeth. One that speaks a different language.

### Supervise kids and dogs

The key to a peaceful household is to socialize your puppy. Early exposure to everything and everyone the dog will need to accept is insurance. Most dogs accept youngsters when they're raised with kids.

Nearly every dog was touted as "tolerant" to "excellent" with kids, even breeds that are extremely large or assertive. Of course, all respondents were experienced, conscientious breeders who take great care to raise trustworthy dogs and to select and advise buyers carefully. I must, however, caution buyers to use their heads.

### Keep your dog busy

Most breeds can participate in performance events if the owner desires. Although some are breed or group specific (lure coursing or herding), several fields are open to all dogs. Any breed can be trained in obedience for house manners if not competition. Well-behaved dogs are able to cheer others by therapy visits. Service-related occupations involve intensive training for the animal. These include dog guides, hearing or wheelchair assistance, military or law enforcement careers.

No matter what the breed, bored dogs are unhappy dogs and will find their own form of entertainment as interior destroyer, neighborhood alarm system or landscape artist. They'll chew, and it probably won't be on your old shoes. Pups always pick the new ones—and the most expensive. They dig. And it won't be in the sandbox or the back corner. It'll be in your rose garden or right smack in front of the door. They howl. And it'll raise the roof . . . and hair on the back of your neighbor's neck. If you're gone long enough, they'll probably decide your living room would make a good bathroom. And it won't be pretty. It'll be in the center of the new beige carpet—more than likely on the same day you bring home guests.

### Enjoy your dog

Just as with kids, the best relationships are developed when you do more than feed, house and holler at them. Loving owners plan time to take a walk or hike (even with that terrific fenced yard), play ball or soccer and show their pet physical affection. Someone who is too busy to do this at least every other day shouldn't have a pet. The dog that regularly receives only food, water and perhaps a treat and a distracted pat on the head may not be neglected, but is not treasured the way a pet should be. If this is the case, why have a dog?

In exchange for half an hour of undivided attention your dog will give you heart, admiration and loyalty forever. This dog will defend you if the need arises. This dog will greet you with glee whenever you come home. This dog will love you without equal.

Over and over again, respondents ended with a phrase similar to: "This is the only breed for me!" Since this occurs with every breed, only one conclusion can be drawn: These people enjoy their dogs! If you do your homework, know what is right for you and find a good breeder, you, too, will find the Perfect Match. Every puppy is only as good as the breeder and you.

# Sporting Dogs

# 3 Be a Sport (Sporting Dogs)

**Sporting dogs** were developed to search for and retrieve gamebirds and water fowl. A few hunt small mammals. They hunt silently, so as not to startle the birds. Although Sporting breeds are sought as eager hunt companions with stamina, many are family dogs, enjoyed for their enthusiasm, gentle temperament and strong desire to please. These are the athletes of the dog world.

Few are couch potatoes (although they might relish a comfy post-game snooze), not well matched with the low-key family that prefers armchair sports to the real thing. They suit joggers and active families who enjoy the outdoors, as well as hunters or Field Trialers. Because Sporting breeds are not notably vocal, neighbors are less likely to find their presence intrusive or annoying. Obedience enthusiasts delight in the group's energy and willingness to please.

These hardy, spirited dogs crave vigorous activity and may create their own indoor gymnasium if not given an energy outlet. Retrievers will happily continue fetching until your arm falls off. With proper exercise, all are easygoing companions. They're social animals and, in addition to play with other dogs, need interaction with their human family.

Sporting dogs are subdivided into four types: pointers, retrievers, setters and spaniels. Each has unique talents and physical characteristics.

**General characteristics:** High energy, friendly, tractable, focused, fun-loving, non-territorial and low protection, a desire to please, not dominant. Often natural retrievers. Must have fencing or other confinement.Their bark is strong and they may cry from boredom.

If you're an active person or have an outlet for an explosion of canine energy, one of the following good sports might be your Perfect Match.

## Brittany

**Size:** Medium, 17.5–20.5", 30–40#

**Color:** Orange and white, liver and white (clear or roaned white)

**Protection:** Alarm barkers, more bark than bite

**Energy:** High

**Life expectancy:** 12 yrs.

**Children:** Gentle, even-tempered, love to play

**Other animals:** Males can be testy with other males

**Abilities:** Bird hunting, Field Trials, Hunting Tests, Obedience

**Shedding/Grooming:** Seasonal / Minimal, brush out dead hair

**Health clearances:** OFA, CERF; **Ask about:** HD, glaucoma, spinal paralysis, seizures, heart and liver problems

**Best with:** Hunters, active families, fenced yards, heart-pumping runs, socialization, Obedience

***Not for:*** Ignoring, handicapped or elderly, small apartments, life in a pen

This Sporting dog was bred to cover a lot of ground. Britts bond closely with those who work them and will do almost anything for that person. Sometimes the Brittany's enthusiasm is so great the result is dismay rather than pleasure.

Determine whether you'd rather have the dog bounce on a brisk walk or on your bed, dart after a squirrel in a fenced area or run from window to window to window. You have a choice: Toss a ball in the backyard, or have it dropped in the middle of the mashed potatoes as an invitation.

## Pointer

**Size:** Large, F. 23–26", 35–65#; M. 25–28", 55–90#; Field Trial lines smaller than show lines

**Color:** Liver, lemon, black, orange, with/without white

**Protection:** Minimal, will bark to alert

**Energy:** Moderate–high; if given opportunity will romp and run all day

**Life expectancy:** 12–14 yrs.

**Children:** Tolerant, playful, loving and protective

**Other animals:** Complacently accept

**Abilities:** Independent, wide-ranging bird dogs; Field Trials, Hunting Tests, Obedience, Tracking, Agility

**Shedding/Grooming:** Seasonal / Minimal, daily brushing with a bristle brush

**Health clearances:** OFA, CERF; **Ask about:** HD, elbow dysplasia, PRA cataracts, entropion; epilepsy

**Best with:** Hunters, active owners, fenced yards, socialization, all-out twice weekly run

***Not for:*** Allergy sufferers, protection

This breed is happiest when having a job to do, whether performance events or home chores, i.e., "Fetch the socks." A home with four teenagers and forty-eight pairs of socks would be heaven to Pointers. If owners don't find a way to channel their urge to work, Pointers might destroy the socks. Birds and other scents excite them, and they're liable to hit the trails by themselves if left unattended. Owners say, "Field Pointers have two passions: birds and food."

While Field lines are hard-headed, show lines are inclined to be soft-natured. When feelings are hurt, they'll pout. These dogs demand attention, craving human companionship. They have an even, sweet temperament and relate best to people of the same demeanor.

## German Shorthaired Pointer

**Size:** Medium, F. 21–23", 45–60#; M. 23–25", 55–70#

**Color:** Liver, liver or white ticked, spotted or roan

**Protection:** Warning (actually "welcoming") bark

**Energy:** High

**Life expectancy:** 14–16 yrs.

**Children:** Loving; exuberance may topple a toddler; eagerly play games and wrestle

**Other animals:** Share well; cat chase is exhilarating

**Abilities:** Hunting, Field Trials, Hunting Tests, Tracking, Obedience, Agility, Flyball, search and rescue

**Shedding/Grooming:** Seasonal in amazing amounts / Minimal, brushing w/rubber curry comb

**Health clearances:** OFA, CERF; **Ask about:** HD, elbow dysplasia, juvenile cataracts, entropion, hypothyroidism, vWD, epilepsy

**Best with:** Hunters, fences, rousing runs and workouts

***Not for:*** Stay-in-beds, frail people, penthouse parties, neglect

Shorthairs are adaptable, tolerant, resilient and happily obedient. They think other dogs are the third best thing in the world, next to their people and birds. During youth, they tremble with barely contained excitement at every bird, falling leaf and breath of wind. A hunt with a Shorthair is often productive.

The breed is as at home in the water as in the field. Admirers say Shorthairs are fun at play, intense at work. "Shorthairs try harder than many other breeds to please their owners."

## German Wirehaired Pointer

**Size:** Medium–large, F. smaller, 22–24", M. 24–26"

**Color:** Solid liver, liver and white; may have spots, roaning, ticking

**Protection:** Medium–high

**Energy:** Medium–high

**Life expectancy:** 10–12 yrs.

**Children:** Good; great sense of humor

**Other animals:** Stands his own with other dogs

**Abilities:** Hunting, retrieving, Field Trials, Hunting Tests, Tracking, Obedience

**Shedding/Grooming:** Seasonal, not heavy/ Regular brushing, hand stripping for show

**Health clearances:** OFA, CERF; **Ask about:** HD, elbow dysplasia, cataracts

**Best with:** Hunters, active owners, training, a sense of humor

***Not for:*** Limited time, snap-to Obedience

Although Wirehairs want to please, they might have their own ideas on how something should be done. Some can be hard-headed. The best owners convince them through firm, gentle persuasion that "People Know Best." Bounce on the front lawn, not the sofa. Play with your toys, not my underwear. Ignore the cat; run the Grand Prix around the furniture if you must, but don't eat the kitty.

This class clown might embarrass owners, but when everyone is through laughing, he could very well become Obedience cum laude. Although Wirehairs can be distracted, once owners have the dogs' attention, they're happy workers.

## Chesapeake Bay Retriever

**Size:** Large, F. 21–24", 55–70#; M. 23–26", 65–80#

**Color:** Browns, from wheaten "deadgrass" to chocolate

**Protection:** High; more territorial than other Sporting dogs

**Energy:** High

**Life expectancy:** 10–12 yrs.

**Children:** Good with considerate ones

**Other animals:** Dominant, but accepting

**Abilities:** Waterfowl retrieving, Hunting Tests, Field Trials, Obedience, Tracking

**Shedding/Grooming:** Seasonal / Brush weekly with rubber curry comb

**Health clearances:** OFA, CERF; **Ask about:** HD*, elbow dysplasia, OCD, PRA

**Best with:** Hunters, early socialization/ Obedience, room for lots of safe exercise, strong leaders

***Not for:*** Novice owners, isolation, inactive people, apartments or condos

Hardy enough to swim for hours in icy waters, Chessies are diehard retrievers driven to perform their quest in life. They LOVE water, swimming, diving and retrieving sticks or birds.

Chessies are strong-willed and protective, more so than the other retrievers. They need a trainer who knows how to gain the dog's respect and admiration. These retrievers work best for someone they love. Owners delight in the breed's trait of grinning and "snickering" when happy or showing submission.

## Curly-Coated Retriever

**Size:** Medium–large, 22–27", 55–75#

**Color:** Black or liver

**Protection:** Alert; good alarm dogs

**Energy:** Very high

**Life expectancy:** 12–13 yrs.

**Children:** Yes, with early socialization and exposure

**Other animals:** Fit into pack smoothly

**Abilities:** Land and water retrievers, Hunting Tests, Obedience, Agility, Flyball

**Shedding/Grooming:** Some / Brush frequently, scissor trim if desired

**Health clearances:** OFA, CERF; **Ask about:** HD, elbow dysplasia, PRA, entropion, cataracts, hypothyroidism, bloat, epilepsy

**Best with:** Hunters, exercise, fenced yards, mental stimuli

***Not for:*** Ignoring, inactive owners

The Curly coat protects the dog from cold and wet weather, and repels water like a mackintosh. Curlies enjoy a damp November day of duck or quail hunting or a snowball fight with the kids. A Curly-Coated Retriever without exercise is a living, breathing example of bouncing off the walls.

The breed is described as as "cheerful, curious, playful, ready for adventure, enthusiastic," attached but not dependent. These dogs make their owners the center of their universe. The Curly-Coated Retriever does not suffer as many problems as plague some of the more popular retrievers.

## Flat-Coated Retriever

**Size:** Medium–large, F. 22–23.5"; M. 23–24.5"

**Color:** Black or liver

**Protection:** Barks alarm, but basically accepts all

**Energy:** High outside; with exercise, quiet indoors

**Life expectancy:** 8–10 yrs.

**Children:** Playful and responsive

**Other animals:** Good-natured

**Abilities:** Upland game hunter and water retriever, Hunting Tests, Obedience, Agility, Flyball

**Shedding/Grooming:** Seasonal / Brushing, some minor trimming

**Health clearances:** OFA, CERF; **Ask about:** HD, patellar luxation, PRA, cataracts, entropion, cancer, hypothyroidism

**Best with:** Hunters, athletic owners, exercise, family life

***Not for:*** Stay-at-homes, invalids, harsh handling

Typical of retrievers, the Flat-Coat is a happy companion and highly trainable and is a good alternative for those who want a dog with the working qualities and temperament of a retriever, but don't want the frequent problems that often accompany a more popular breed.

This Retriever is a diligent worker, eagerly diving into thick brush or icy water to retrieve his quarry. Flat-Coats are considered extremely birdy in the field.

## Golden Retriever

**Size:** Medium, F. 21.5–22.5", 55–65#; M. 23–24", 65–75#

**Color:** Pale to reddish gold

**Protection:** Poor, will bark (in joyful anticipation of company)

**Energy:** Moderately high, Field lines higher than show lines

**Life expectancy:** 10–14 yrs.

**Children:** Extremely loving and patient; some may be too rowdy for infants or toddlers

**Other animals:** Love to play, tolerate most, often roll over first; some studs object to sharing with other males

**Abilities:** Obedience, Agility, Flyball, search and rescue, Field Trials, Hunting Tests, service fields, therapy, hunting

**Shedding/Grooming:** Yes, profuse / Brushing twice a week

**Health clearances:** OFA, CERF; **Ask about:** vWD, HD*, OCD, cataracts, entropion, SAS, hypothyroidism, epilepsy

**Best with:** Fences, active, social people

***Not for:*** Watch dog, backyard life, small apartments, allergic owners, fussy house-keepers

Goldens tackle everything with a passion. This is a mega-dog, "lots of hair, lots of energy, lots of love." And lots of food. Vets say Goldens will eat themselves into blimps. Measured meals rather than self-feeding keeps them trim. As with all popular breeds, special care must be taken when looking for a pup. All that glitters is not Golden. Dogs are only as good as their breeders.

The breed's Obedience capabilities are legendary. Goldens are trusting, biddable, consistent, happy and often precise workers. Their gentleness and willingness to throw their shoulders into a job make them a top choice for assistance dogs.

## Labrador Retriever

**Size:** Large, F. 21.5–23.5", 55–70#; M. 22.5–24.5", 6–80#

**Color:** Black, chocolate, yellow

**Protection:** Alarm barker

**Energy:** High, especially in puppyhood

**Life expectancy:** 10 yrs.

**Children:** Patient; large, exuberant puppy can overwhelm timid or little ones

**Other animals:** Amiable

**Abilities:** Hunting and retrieving, Obedience, Field Trials, Hunting Tests, service fields, therapy

**Shedding/Grooming:** Moderate and seasonal / Groom with slicker brush, clean ears frequently

**Health clearances:** OFA, CERF; **Ask about:** HD, elbow dysplasia, OCD, CMO, PRA, cataracts and other eye problems, diabetes, epilepsy, hypothyroidism, vWD

**Best with:** Active owners, Obedience training, secure fencing

***Not for:*** Remote control surfers, neatniks

Born to swim, the Lab's love for water can be dangerous to a dog unable to climb out of a swimming pool. Owners are cautioned to prevent pool access except when they are with the dog.

A well-bred Lab is sturdy, able to follow human companions through woods, hill and dale, then jump into icy waters to retrieve. When Labs are determined and set to a certain task, it's sometimes difficult to convince them otherwise. Thus, there is a need to teach manners to this happy, powerful, self-willed dog early in puppyhood. The breed's popularity has attracted unscrupulous and unknowledgeable breeders, leading to health and temperament problems. Going to a person who has "just bred the family pet" can wind up costing a great deal more in veterinary bills and peace of mind.

## English Setter

Photo: Graham

**Size:** Medium–large, F. 24", M. 25"

**Color:** Orange, blue, lemon or liver belton (white with colored flecks or roan shading), tricolor

**Protection:** Will bark at strangers, but friendly

**Energy:** Moderately high, need leg-stretching walks

**Life expectancy:** 10–12 yrs.

**Children:** Excellent, may be too exuberant for little ones

**Other animals:** Good rapport

**Abilities:** Upland bird hunting, Hunting Tests, therapy, field lines—Field Trials

**Shedding/Grooming:** Yes / Brush every couple of days

**Health clearances:** OFA, CERF, BAER; **Ask about:** HD*, elbow dysplasia, cancer, hypothyroidism, deafness

**Best with:** Affectionate owners, casual households, stimulating runs

***Not for:*** Guarding, loud households, snap-to Obedience, fussy housekeepers

These astute, sweet-natured dogs read their people well. They'll rough-and-tumble with teens, gently kiss toddlers, run with one adult and quietly lie at the feet of another. Bred to cover large areas, they are steady, eager, energetic hunting companions, willing to continue as long as their master wants.

The "English gentleman" is always a mannerly companion. They are "overly anxious to please, which might irritate some people." For a large dog, they are surprisingly graceful. One of the most appealing aspects of this setter is its stable, easygoing temperament.

## Gordon Setter

**Size:** Large, F. 23–26", 45–70#; M. 24–27", 55–80#

**Color:** Black with tan (mahogany or chestnut) markings

**Protection:** Good alarm dogs, unlikely to back it up

**Energy:** High; calmer when mature

**Life expectancy:** 10–12 yrs.

**Children:** Enthusiastic wagging can topple toddlers; may be protective

**Other animals:** Friendly, but like to take charge

**Abilities:** Pointing upland game birds, Obedience, Field Trials, Hunting Tests, Agility, therapy

**Shedding/Grooming:** Yes! / Daily brushing prevents mats and eliminates dead hair

**Health clearances:** OFA, CERF; **Ask about:** HD*, PRA, bloat, hypothyroidism

**Best with:** Fencing, active owners; firm, consistent training

***Not for:*** Neatniks, easily intimidated people, harsh handling, allergy sufferers, long hours alone

A daily three-mile walk plus a short run are recommended for a peaceful household. The Gordon Setter rescue organization warns owners, "Sitting in a backyard alone does not count as exercise." Hunters find them affable, hard-working companions in the field, willing to keep going all day if asked. Gordons work best in a one-on-one partnership. They tend to hunt more closely than the other setters, advantageous for the occasional weekend hunting enthusiast.

The breed likes to be in charge and, given a chance to be top dog, a Gordon will take it. Silly and entertaining one moment, regal and dignified the next, small wonder they're touted as having beauty, brains and bird sense.

## Irish Setter

**Size:** Large, F. 25", 60#; M. 27", 70#

**Color:** Mahogany or chestnut red

**Protection:** Low, but announce visitors

**Energy:** High, exuberant

**Life expectancy:** 12–14 yrs

**Children:** Yes, may be too boisterous for toddlers; always ready for a game and sloppy kisses

**Other animals:** Interact well

**Abilities:** Upland bird hunting, retrieving, Field Trials, Hunting Tests, Obedience, Agility, therapy

**Shedding/Grooming:** Seasonal / Brush weekly at least, more during shed; pet owners might clip under ears and armpits

**Health clearances:** OFA, CERF (or DNA for PRA); **Ask about:** Hypothyroidism, epilepsy, bloat

**Best with:** Patient, undemanding owners with a sense of humor; consistent, soft training methods

***Not for:*** Inactive or allergic people

The flashy, happy-go-lucky redhead has suffered a reputation for being hyperactive. After all, these dogs were bred to run on a hunt all day. Common sense says they aren't going to be happy locked in a house all day, then be content with a stroll to the nearest tree. A fenced area and two to three long, vigorous walks or play sessions will keep their high energy under control. Puppies and untrained adults can be mischievous and hard-headed. Although Irish Setters do show bird instinct, they are not as popular with hunters, in part because of the heavier coat.

Irish Setters work best for someone who is willing to be patient, gaining their attention and interest. They're sensitive and really want to please, but sometimes the bird in the bush is more intriguing. These dogs are natural clowns, aptly described in their breed Standard as "rollicking."

## American Water Spaniel

**Size:** Medium, 15–18", F. 25–40#; M. 30–45#

**Color:** Solid liver, brown, dark chocolate

**Protection:** Good watchdog

**Energy:** High as youngsters

**Life expectancy:** 10–15 yrs.

**Children:** Very good, but expose when young

**Other animals:** Enjoys other pets, will drive strange canines away

**Abilities:** Hunting, retrieving, Tracking, Obedience

**Shedding/Grooming:** Light, but constant / Brush weekly; clip excess hair from feet, topknot and top of ears; clean ears

**Health clearances:** OFA, CERF; **Ask about:** Patellar luxation, PRA, detached retina, cataracts, epilepsy, hypothyroidism

**Best with:** Upland birds or waterfowl hunters, active families, lots of attention

***Not for:*** Inactive people, first-time dog owners, the yard-proud, those lacking time

Although not a common breed, the AWS is a sturdy, enthusiastic hunting companion, happily retrieving. Of course, true to their name, these dogs take to the water like the feathered game they seek. Owners say the breed has great instinct and possesses great heart for the hunt.

Obedience should be a prerequisite to show the youngster just who fetches the slippers. Bored and left alone, they're liable to dig or bark happily while chasing squirrels and birds around the yard. American Water Spaniels mature slowly; owners shouldn't expect too much too soon.

## Clumber Spaniel

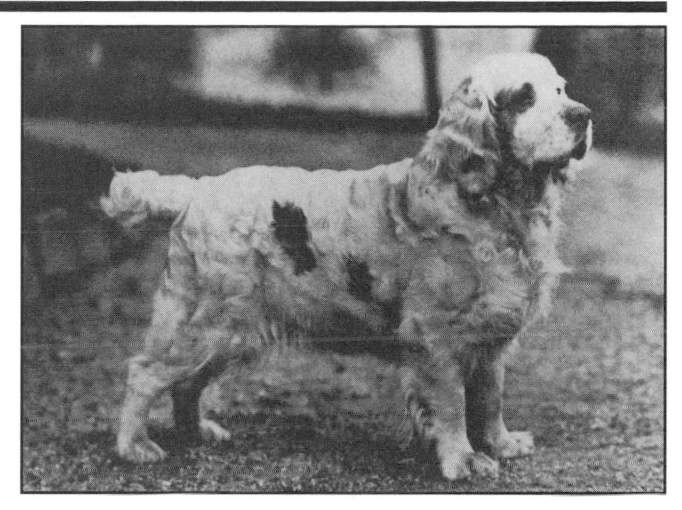

**Size:** Medium, F. 17–19", 55–70#; M. 19–20", 70–85#

**Color:** White with lemon or orange markings

**Protection:** Nearly nonexistent, but will bark

**Energy:** Medium

**Life expectancy:** 10+ yrs

**Children:** Very good even when not exposed to them

**Other animals:** Usually accepting

**Abilities:** Tracking, hunting

**Shedding/Grooming:** Definitely / Daily brushing, clean ears, occasionally trim bottom of feet; pets' feathering may be clipped

**Health clearances:** OFA, CERF; **Ask about:** Cataracts, entropion or ectropion, vertebral disk problems, HD*

**Best with:** Hunters, social people, fenced yards

***Not for:*** Neatniks, jogging companions, high jumps

Although the breed has enough stamina to join a hunter, take long hikes or participate in Tracking, the Clumber is a steady, silent worker rather than a spirited one. A flushing breed, they can move close to game. The sleepy appearance changes markedly to wide awake at the scent of birds.

Admirers say they are "aristocratic, charming, loving, entertaining, inquisitive, affectionate, intelligent, gentle, mischievous, stubborn, determined, self-willed, appealing and naughty." Because of low numbers in the breed, prospective buyers must be prepared to wait. The dog's structure combined with the small gene pool means few Clumbers boast good OFA ratings. Reputable breeders radiograph and breed accordingly in order to upgrade. Look for lines that have been x-rayed for several generations with improvement.

## Cocker Spaniel (American)

**Size:** Small, F. 14.5", 22–25#; M. 15.5", 25–28#

**Color:** Black, buff, red, chocolate, black and tan; particolors—black, red or chocolate with white; tricolor

**Protection:** Maybe—but don't count on it

**Energy:** Medium–high

**Life expectancy:** 10–14 yrs.

**Children:** Yes, but check out pup's parents and avoid timid or snappy

**Other animals:** Sociable and gentle

**Abilities:** Retrieving, Hunting Tests, Agility, Obedience, Flyball

**Shedding/Grooming:** Yes / Preferably daily brushing, trim and bathe every couple of months; clean ears frequently

**Health clearances:** OFA, CERF; **Ask about:** HD, PRA, cataracts, autoimmune diseases, epilepsy, skin conditions

**Best with:** Loving, sociable owners; those into hair care

***Not for:*** Backyard life, serious hunters

Cockers have been among the top ten breeds in registrations for many years—and with good reason. Their temperament is described as "merry," and jovial they are. They're also curious, playful and occasionally stubborn.

With the popularity comes breed warnings. Search out sincere, dedicated breeders who really care about maintaining the breed, its health and a playful, sunny temperament. Few people hunt with Cockers although they can be trained to flush and retrieve.

## English Cocker Spaniel

**Size:** Medium, F. 15–16", 26–32#; M. 16–17", 28–34#

**Color:** White with black, blue, liver or red markings, roaning or ticking; black, liver or red with/without tan markings

**Protection:** Will alert

**Energy:** High as puppies, medium as they age

**Life expectancy:** 12–15 yrs.

**Children:** Usually adore them; good size for kids

**Other animals:** With adequate introduction

**Abilities:** Hunting, Hunting Tests, Agility, Obedience, Tracking

**Shedding/Grooming:** Year-round / Brushing weekly or more often; some clipping and scissoring; hand stripping for show; frequent ear care

**Health clearances:** OFA, CERF; **Ask about:** HD, PRA, cataracts, kidney disease, deafness

**Best with:** Social people, sense of humor; gentle but firm enforcement of rules

***Not for:*** Wishy-washy disciplinarians, backyard life, the houseproud or allergic

Spaniels are all social dogs, real party animals. Those who want a decorative pet and don't want a busy, tagalong buddy should avoid this breed. They always greet their owners with delight and abandon whether they've been gone ten minutes or ten hours.

Most show Field instinct, but if hunting is a priority, owners should look to Field lines with more drive. Usually eager to please, some can be willful. If allowed, they might become overpossessive with toys. Early reminders teach them to share and that people rule the household.

## English Springer Spaniel

Photo: Downey

**Size:** Medium, F. 19", 40#; M. 20", 50#

**Color:** Black and white, liver and white, or tricolored; may have ticking

**Protection:** Noisy watchdog

**Energy:** Medium high–high

**Life expectancy:** 12 yrs.

**Children:** Great playmates; choose friendly, outgoing lines

**Other animals:** Usually good

**Abilities:** Flushing upland gamebirds, Field Trials, Hunting Tests, Obedience, Agility, Flyball, Tracking, therapy

**Shedding/Grooming:** Seasonal / Brushing, some trimming; clean ears frequently

**Health clearances:** OFA, CERF; **Ask about:** HD, PRA, ectropion, glaucoma, retinal dysplasia, epilepsy, vWD, SAS

**Best with:** Regular exercise and grooming, fenced yard

***Not for:*** Sedentary people, small apartments

English Springer show and Field lines started with the same basic dog and then reached a fork in the road. Breeders usually concentrate their interests on one area, although a few compete and can boast wins in both.

The deeper-bodied show Springer is more compact with heavier bone than his field cousin. The thicker coat requires more care. Show lines are not as high-charged as the Field pup and may be better for the family that isn't interested in hunting urges. Field lines can be leggier and more racey, with less coat and glamour. They're intense, energetic, enthusiastic workers. The majority of Springers are "good-time Charlies," happy to play the clown and bring cheer to their owners' lives.

## Field Spaniel

**Size:** Medium, F. 17"; M. 18"

**Color:** Black, liver, golden liver, roan

**Protection:** Alarm bark

**Energy:** High, enthusiastic about everything

**Life expectancy:** 10–12 yrs.

**Children:** Yes, loves everyone; always ready to play games

**Other animals:** Easygoing, relates well to housemates

**Abilities:** Hunting, Tracking, Agility, Obedience, Hunting Tests

**Shedding/Grooming:** Heavy / Frequent brushing, trimming head, ears, neck and tail

**Health clearances:** OFA, CERF; **Ask about:** HD*, PRA, cataracts, hypothyroidism

**Best with:** Hunters, training, quick thinkers, outdoor lovers

***Not for:*** House Beautiful fanatics, inactive people

Strong instinct, ability and endurance make Field Spaniels great flushing dogs and hunting companions. But they are just as happy taking a hike if that's the preference.

Tolerance of the breed's enthusiastic lifestyle and the ability to laugh are important ownership requirements. Too busy to pause, the Field gulps water, leaving pools along the floor, and slobbering the rest on your leg when coming to share your love. (Or is it a clever maneuver to dry his mouth?) Owners are happy this even-tempered, friendly dog might be dogdom's best-kept secret!

## Irish Water Spaniel

Photo: J. Ashbey

**Size:** Medium, F. 21–23", 45–60#; M. 22–24", 55–65#

**Color:** Liver

**Protection:** Excellent at alerting, reserved with strangers

**Energy:** High as puppy

**Life expectancy:** 10–12 yrs.

**Children:** Yes; gentle, good guardian

**Other animals:** Accept with aplomb; some studs bristle at other males

**Abilities:** Hunting, retrieving, Hunting Tests, Obedience, Field Trials, Tracking, Agility, service fields

**Shedding/Grooming:** Minimal / Good for allergic owners; brushing twice a week; some trimming

**Health clearances:** OFA, CERF; **Ask about:** vWD; HD, autoimmune diseases, hypothyroidism, epilepsy

**Best with:** Hunters, outdoor enthusiasts, sense of humor

***Not for:*** Those who hate grooming or have little play time

This, the largest Spaniel, boasts the characteristics of several canine families: the affection of a spaniel, the fetching instinct of the retrievers, a coat similar to a Poodle, a love of water and the spirit of a true Sporting dog. Although the breed is not commonplace, hunters swear by its retrieving abilities. The bold, dashing Irish is a powerful swimmer and strongly built with rugged endurance.

IWSs have a good sense of humor. They like to know what people are doing and are likely to stick their noses around the shower curtain.

## Sussex Spaniel

**Size:** Small–medium, 13–15", 35–45#

**Color:** Rich golden liver

**Protection:** Vigorously protect property

**Energy:** Medium

**Life expectancy:** 11–12 yrs.

**Children:** Good guardians, especially if raised with them

**Other animals:** Friendly, but like to run the show

**Abilities:** Hunting, Tracking

**Shedding/Grooming:** Average / Easy care, brushing, occasional trimming

**Health clearances:** OFA; **Ask about:** HD*, autoimmune diseases, heart defects, hypothyroidism

**Best with:** Patient, loving owners, a good mix of outdoor/indoor togetherness, Obedience, socialization

***Not for:*** Ignoring, joggers, instant action and reaction

A rarity in the Sporting group, Sussex enjoy snoring by owners' feet as much as playing ball or an outing. Not speed demons, they are methodical, determined workers.

Although they appear as somber as a parson, they're cheerful and friendly with a good sense of humor. Due to a small gene pool, hip dysplasia and hypothyroidism have not been easy to weed out. But conscientious breeders are striving to correct and decrease the numbers of these conditions. Look for lines that are continually upgrading. Sussex are not easy to breed and tricky to raise to 12–14 weeks; thus, puppies are only rarely available.

## Welsh Springer Spaniel

**Size:** Medium, 35–45#, F. 17–18"; M. 18–19"

**Color:** Red and white

**Protection:** Alarm bark, but turn to mush when people enter

**Energy:** High as puppy, mellow out a bit in age

**Life expectancy:** 12–14 yrs.

**Children:** Gentle, some are cautious

**Other animals:** Ignore or tolerate other pets

**Abilities:** Hunting, Obedience, Hunting Tests, Agility, Tracking

**Shedding/Grooming:** Yes / Brushing weekly, trim feathering as needed

**Health clearances:** OFA, CERF; **Ask about:** HD*, PRA, cataracts, glaucoma, epilepsy

**Best with:** Those who enjoy lots of doggy hugs and kisses

***Not for:*** Time constraints, touch-me-nots, outdoor living

Welsh love a run, but don't require as much exercise as many other Sporting breeds. They like to know where you are, but they'll calmly watch from the couch as owners bustle about their duties. This Welshman cannot stand being excluded from activities. One jumped off an elevated porch to follow an owner. Their total worship may unnerve some people.

This doesn't mean Welsh Springers don't welcome rough-and-tumble games. And they'll eagerly tackle any turf or dive in any water. Field or show dog, this breed happily crosses over into the other's territory. Their sweet expressions first attract people. But the inner gentleness and their sensitivity are what sell owners on the breed.

## Vizsla

**Size:** Medium, F. 21–23"; M. 22–24"

**Color:** Golden rust

**Protection:** Low (some lines are more territorial)

**Energy:** High

**Life expectancy:** 11–14 yrs.

**Children:** Most are O.K.

**Other animals:** Usually

**Abilities:** Upland bird hunting, Field Trials, Hunting Tests, Tracking, Obedience, Agility

**Shedding/Grooming:** Yes, constant floor sweeping / Hair sticks tight to everything; wash-and-wear, easy-care

**Health clearances:** OFA, CERF, skin punch for SA; **Ask about:** HD, PRA, entropion, SA, epilepsy

**Best with:** Active people, joggers, hunters, Obedience

***Not for:*** Remote control addicts, long spans alone, trigger tempers

Typical of the Pointer clan, Vizslas are high-energy dogs that demand attention and want ACTION! Outdoor fencing is a must as their body and brain say "Go, go go!" at every bird or scent. A quick, highly skilled pointer, the Vizsla is usually a close working gun dog.

A great buddy for the athlete, the Vizsla might be a bit busy for those who view a walk to the car as their daily exercise. The proper temperament is gentle, sensitive, yet fearless. The Vizsla is as eager to join in the fun at age eleven, as during puppyhood.

## Weimaraner

**Size:** Large, F. 23–25", 50–70#; M. 25–27", 70–85#

**Color:** Mouse gray to silver gray

**Protection:** Moderately high

**Energy:** HIGH!

**Life expectancy:** 10–12 yrs.

**Children:** Yes, but may topple toddlers

**Other animals:** Social, males sometimes grumble at others; cats are temptations

**Abilities:** Game bird pointing and retrieving, Field Trials, Hunting Tests, Obedience, Agility, Tracking and trailing, Flyball, search and rescue, service fields

**Shedding/Grooming:** Minimal / Daily brushing

**Health clearances:** OFA, CERF; **Ask about:** HD, elbow dysplasia, HOD, PRA, entropion, bleeding disorders, torsion, spinal disease, heart defects

**Best with:** Hunters or outdoorsy, active, confident owners; Obedience training

***Not for:*** Sedentary, lazy trainers; long periods alone

Weims can hunt as long as six hours at a time. This kind of energy will explode if the dog is expected to be content with a stroll around the block and a once-a-day pat on the head. The Weim's sturdiness and stamina are what appeal to some, turn off others. At one time used for big game hunting, today's game might be birds or Frisbees.

Weims can be stubborn, so it's best to establish who's boss. They love being challenged with training and chores but, if allowed, will do things their way—like going through the screen door instead of the doggie door.

## Wirehaired Pointing Griffon

**Size:** Medium–large

**Color:** Chestnut, solid or with roaning

**Protection:** Will bark; won't start trouble, but capable of finishing it

**Energy:** Moderate, with regular runs content inside

**Life expectancy:** 12–15 yrs.

**Children:** Yes, but consider kids their equals—children have to earn respect to gain cooperation

**Other animals:** Play well once pecking order is established; cats are in for a chase

**Abilities:** Upland bird and waterfowl hunting, Agility, Hunting Tests, Flyball, Obedience, search and rescue, therapy

**Shedding/Grooming:** Minimal / Weekly brushing, hand stripping for show; frequent facial shampoos

**Health clearances:** OFA, CERF; **Ask about:** HD, ectropion, entropion

**Best with:** Secure fencing, joggers, hunters, outdoor activity

***Not for:*** The housebound, harsh handling, backyard life, apartment dwellers

It takes searching to find a Griffon breeder. Enthusiastic owners wonder why, as the Griffon is a loving family dog and a versatile pointer. Solid, dependable hunters, these dogs tend to work within gun range, pointing and retrieving upland birds. Although they are capable in Field Trials, they are not competitive with wider-ranging Brittanys, setters and pointers. With the protective coat, they'll happily retrieve in water as well. Breeders promote natural hunting instincts and prefer to sell to those who will encourage it.

As a rule, the breed has a sensitive nature and wants to please, but can be stubborn and independent. Strong, but not too macho to show their soft side, Griffons occasionally can be impish.

# Hounds

4

# To the Hounds! (Hounds)

All dogs have a superior sense of smell. **Hounds** can boast the best of the best. This group includes the Scenthounds and Sighthounds.

The **Scenthounds'** preeminent sense of smell makes their world an exciting sensorial potpourri. Their perceptive noses seek game from rabbits and squirrels to otters, elk and mountain lions. Some track their prey by air scenting, others follow a ground trail. Since they work some distance from the hunter, they fill the air with a resounding bay to mark their location. Hounds are more independent than Sporting dogs, ranging far from their masters as they seek their quarry.

Scenthounds are social creatures. As they often worked in packs originally, they ran, lived, slept and played together. Even today, hunters often hit the trail with more than one hound. This sociability makes them easy to be around. These loving hounds accept people and other dogs with easy aplomb, although cats or small pets might be perceived as prey.

The **Sighthounds** (or Gazehounds) are the swiftest canines. They aren't expected to take direction from their master, but to sight and chase a fleeing animal. In the modern world, Sighthounds are rarely used for hunting. Instead, their fleet feet might beat the turf, chasing a lure. Many enjoy running with their human partners. Sighthounds are particularly sensitive to anesthetics because of less body fat in proportion to bone and muscle. Be sure to discuss this with a veterinarian prior to any procedure requiring anesthesia.

Hound size ranges from the tallest canine, the Irish Wolfhound, to the diminutive Miniature Dachshund. Temperaments can be feisty like the Dachshunds and Elkhounds, sweet and mellow like the Coonhounds or aloof like the desert hounds. Some hounds not only trailed their prey, but brought it down or fought it underground. Wolves, boars, lions and badgers would have made meatloaf of timid dogs. Bred to hunt without commands, hounds aren't for people who want instant response or robot dogs.

Although hounds have plenty of stamina, they're not as wired as the Sporting group. Many will gladly warm up the couch for you if allowed. In addition to hunters, they're great companions for runners, power walkers and people who want to throw a ball for a bit, then curl up with their dog at their feet.

**General characteristics:** Independent, excellent senses, non-territorial, not dominant. Happier with instinct outlet. Possess strong chase instinct—need confinement. **Scenthounds:** adaptable, accepting, social, bold; **Sighthounds:** quiet, placid, aloof.

Bark: Scenthounds bay and often raise their voices in song; Sighthounds alarm bark.

## Afghan Hound

**Size:** Large, F. 25"; M. 26–28"

**Color:** Any color

**Protection:** Will bark

**Energy:** High as youngsters; need daily heart-pounding gallop

**Life expectancy:** 10–12 yrs.

**Children:** Some are aloof

**Other animals:** Friendly, establish pecking order; cats and small game become endangered species

**Abilities:** Lure coursing, hunters in homeland

**Shedding/Grooming:** Yes / Extensive with pin brush, 3–4 hrs. a week, use detanglers; mats if neglected

**Health clearances:** OFA, CERF, **Ask about:** HD, cataracts, hypothyroidism, autoimmune diseases

**Best with:** Active people, fenced yards, wannabe hairdressers, early socialization

***Not for:*** Lazy groomers, rigid trainers, people who want instant affection and docile compliance

Bred to hunt deer and leopards, the elegant Afghans are not wimps. They were bred for stamina to run ahead of mounted hunters. Agile and swift, Afghans leap and turn with grace. Owners must be patient in winning the dog's respect, attention and affection. Independent thinkers, Afghans choose when to come and when to respond. These dogs are neither fawning nor demanding, and tend to remain aloof, particularly with strangers.

Their on-again, off-again appetites may need the temptation of yogurt, chicken or garlic powder. But don't let them make you Chief Cook. Despite their pickiness, Afghans have a touch of larceny in their hearts and might steal the toast out of the toaster. Snoods help keep their ear fringes from dangling in the food.

## Basenji

**Size:** Small, F. 16", 22#; M. 17", 24#

**Color:** Chestnut red, black, black and tan, or brindle with white markings

**Protection:** Courage beyond his size

**Energy:** Medium

**Life expectancy:** 13 yrs.

**Children:** Yes

**Other animals:** Love to play

**Abilities:** Lure coursing, Obedience, Agility, hunting, Tracking

**Shedding/Grooming:** Minimal, extremely clean / A lick and a whistle does it

**Health clearances:** OFA, CERF; **Ask about:** PRA and other eye defects, malabsorption, PKD, Fanconi's Syndrome

**Best with:** Active families, cat lovers, fences

***Not for:*** Backyard dog, a push-button mentality

The Basenji, often called the barkless dog, is by no means noiseless. Although silent workers, these Sighthounds break into a joyful yodel during play and when greeting owners. Basenji curiosity can cause trouble. Perky and spirited, they love to be in the middle of things and won't accept no for an answer. Basenjis think situations are made for their entertainment, as in: "Hmmmm, a hole—I'd better explore. Let's make it bigger! A laundry basket—they must want me to empty it. A box of tissue—I'll make confetti."

Basenjis have no fear of cars and hit the chase gear if allowed. Catlike, they're fastidious in their grooming habits, licking themselves clean. They love to climb and are often found on top of the strangest places. Basenjis are friendly, but prefer to make the first advances. Their wrinkled brow gives a bit of a worried look, which owners know is a facade, for the world is their oyster.

## Basset Hound

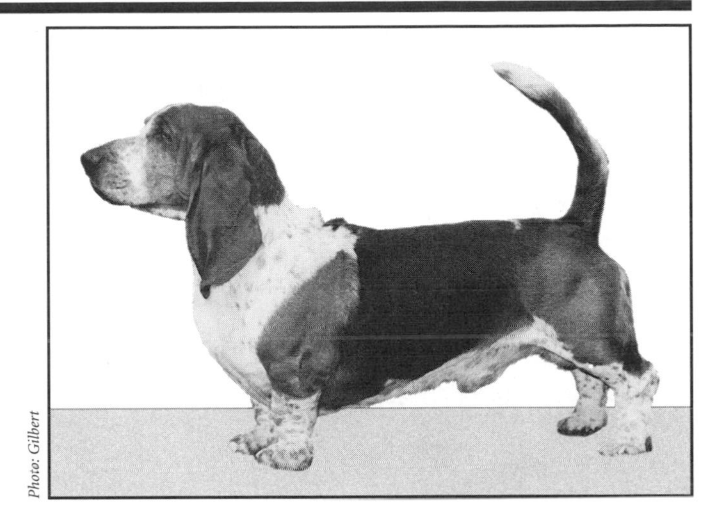
*Photo: Gilbert*

**Size:** Medium, but heavy boned, 40–80#, F. 14"; M. 15"

**Color:** Black, tan with white markings, red with white, piebald

**Protection:** Low; will bark, but loves everybody

**Energy:** Low, but durable; laid back in house, but can hunt all day; playful pups

**Life expectancy:** 12 yrs.

**Children:** Enjoy them, even-tempered

**Other animals:** Social and usually easygoing

**Abilities:** Tracking, Field Trials, rabbit hunting

**Shedding/Grooming:** Moderate / Brush, clean ears often

**Health clearances:** OFA, CERF; **Ask about:** OCD, patellar luxation, elbow dysplasia, PRA, ectropion, entropion, glaucoma, epilepsy, torsion, spinal disease, bleeding disorders, vWD

**Best with:** Fenced yard, dog-oriented people

***Not for:*** Fussbudget housekeepers, snap-to-it demands

Bassets are notably friendly and adaptable. But these Hounds can be stubborn and require a patient trainer, preferably with a pocket full of goodies. Bassets tend to be tunnel-visioned when following a scent. The breed's Tracking skills are second only to the Bloodhound. This can lead them to trouble, loss or death if not confined.

Their big feet, trailing ears and low-slung undersides pick up dirt and carry it with them. They'll also drink and slobber across the floor. Bassets are willing to play the clown, but at their own choosing.

## Beagle

**Size:** Small, two varieties—13" and under, over 13–15", 16–30#

**Color:** Usually black and tan, red or lemon, with or without white markings

**Protection:** Bark at strangers, can be territorial

**Energy:** Medium, play when invited, quiet inside

**Life expectancy:** 10–14 yrs.

**Children:** Expose early, then patient and tolerant

**Other animals:** Social, easygoing

**Abilities:** Hunting, Field Trials, Agility, Scent Hurdles, Flyball

**Shedding/Grooming:** Year-round / Slick with a hound glove, clean ears often

**Health clearances:** OFA, CERF; **Ask about:** Glaucoma, cataracts, retinal atrophy, hypothyroidism, epilepsy, intervertebral disk disease

**Best with:** Active playmates, secure fencing with no access for digging

***Not for:*** The yard-proud, instant Obedience, people irritated by barking or enthusiastic AROOOOO

Curiosity kills not only cats, but Beagles too if it leads them into traffic or to disappear. With their acute sense of smell, sometimes their noses tempt them into trouble. Fence lines must be secured by cement, shrubbery or other discouragement to excavation. Beagles are persistent and have an independent streak, but once they understand you're the boss, they're content to follow. These hardy, affectionate dogs can be clowns. "The only other selfless love that comes close is a mother's. And even she gets mad at you sometimes."

Food training works well, as these hounds aren't above snitching a sandwich from an eye-level plate. "Beagles can convince you they're starving when they just finished off a 20-pound bag of dog food." The breed is prone to obesity and consequent problems, such as disk disorders.

## Black & Tan Coonhound

Photo: Kohler

**Size:** Large, 65–100#, F. 23–25"; M. 25–27"

**Color:** Black with tan markings

**Protection:** Yes, will bark; will protect if pressed

**Energy:** Moderate, when invited will join fun

**Life expectancy:** 10–12 yrs.

**Children:** Very good

**Other animals:** Accept with waggy nonchalance; may chase cats

**Abilities:** Hunting, Coonhound Trials

**Shedding/Grooming:** Yes / Easy, with rubber curry comb; frequent ear cleaning

**Health clearances:** OFA, CERF; **Ask about:** HD, PRA, cataracts, ectropion, bleeding disorders

**Best with:** Secure confinement, hunters

***Not for:*** High-scoring Obedience dreams

Truly an all-American breed, Coonhounds are mellow, laid back and easygoing. Their gentle temperament suits the family looking for a pet that is unintrusive, but there when needed. They're affectionate, but aren't pests about it. Coonhounds are definite couch spuds; owners might have to fight for a seat.

But put them on a scent, and they're hot on the trail, giving voice with a hearty bay every inch of the way, changing tone upon reaching their quarry. Owners can tell their own dog's voice miles away at night, distinguishing it from the entire pack. Although Coonhounds have an inborn drive to tree raccoons, they'll scent out small game, deer or even bear and large "cats."

## Bloodhound

Photo: Gilbert

**Size:** Large, 80–110#, F. 23–25"; M. 25–27"

**Color:** Black and tan, red and tan, tawny

**Protection:** A big bass bark can be followed up if pushed

**Energy:** Once youthful vigor winds down, becomes image of ol' hound dawg snorin' on the porch

**Life expectancy:** 7–9 yrs.

**Children:** Most tolerate kids clambering around them; size can be a problem with small children

**Other animals:** Social

**Abilities:** Tracking par excellence, search and rescue

**Shedding/Grooming:** Seasonal / Brush and clean ears frequently

**Health clearances:** OFA, CERF; **Ask about:** HD*, elbow dysplasia, bloat, torsion, entropion, ectropion

**Best with:** Secure fences, firm loving direction, exercise

***Not for:*** House Beautiful, pushovers, precious objets d'art

Owners warn that Bloodhounds seem to become deaf and blind when on a trail. "They run into things and ignore your calls." Those long, hanging ears sweep intoxicating aromas into large nostrils. And the capacious nose is at the right level for an embarrassing crotch sniff of guests.

The wagging Bloodhound tail is deemed a lethal weapon. Fanciers secure breakable items above tail height and accept bruised shins as part of having a happy dog. A vigorous shake of the hound's head flips drool onto furniture, clothing or the ceiling. Owners have to steel their nerves to the big, sad eyes and be firm. An owner says, "Ours don't know *we* have any friends, they think everyone's coming to see *them.* But not every individual is as friendly." If not, buyers could be sleeping on the porch while the hound curls up on the bed.

## Borzoi

**Size:** Large, F 26–30", 65–85#; M 28–33", 85–110#

**Color:** Any color, with or without markings

**Protection:** Low; rarely bark, but size is a deterrent

**Energy:** Laid back indoors; a couple of brisk walks daily

**Life expectancy:** 8–13 yrs.

**Children:** Some; size may be a problem with tiny tots

**Other animals:** Enjoy dogs, but furry, fast-moving creatures might be seen as game

**Abilities:** Lure coursing

**Shedding/Grooming:** Seasonal / Few minutes daily brushing with pin brush; mats if neglected

**Health clearances:** OFA, CERF; **Ask about:** PRA, cataracts, retinopathy, bloat, cardiac disease, bone cancer, toxin and anesthesia sensitivity

**Best with:** Fenced yard, exercise space, cool place in heat

***Not for:*** Heavy-handed or high-strung owners, lack of time, long periods crated

Borzoi are quiet and graceful as long as they have an occasional opportunity to race the wind. With their built-in fur coats, Borzoi love to play in the cold. Although the breed chased down wolves, thus the alias Russian Wolfhound, they rarely hunt today. Their eagle eyes can spy a far-away critter and the dog is gone in an instant, with no thought to cars or other danger.

The extremely deep chest means a predisposition to bloat. Good animal management calls for dividing food allotment into two meals, as well as limiting exercise and water intake before and after eating.

## Dachshund

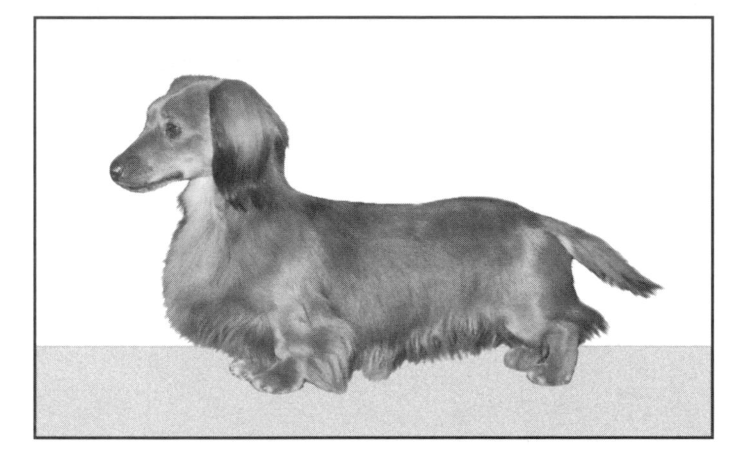

**Size:** Small, Miniature <11#, Standard 20–28#

**Color:** Sable, chocolate, black and tan, chocolate and tan, all with or without brindling or merling (dapples)

**Protection:** Alert, will bark—a lot, if allowed

**Energy:** Medium–high

**Life expectancy:** 12–14 yrs.

**Children:** Longhairs very good, Wirehairs good, Smooths fairly good; Miniatures with older children

**Other animals:** Some co-exist peacefully, many are bossy; death on rodents

**Abilities:** Earthdog Tests, Field Trials, Tracking, Obedience, hunting

**Shedding/Grooming:** Seasonal, smooth and wire lose minimal hair / Brush, some trimming on longhaired; stripping like terrier for wire

**Health clearances:** OFA, CERF; **Ask about:** Elbow dysplasia, patellar luxation, PRA, cataracts, diabetes, epilepsy, intervertebral disk disease, other spinal problems

**Best with:** Consistent and patient training, confident owners, sense of humor

***Not for:*** High jumping, allergic people, prize gardeners, those who wish the ultimate Obedience dog; small kids with Minis

Dachsies are as much terriers as hounds, feisty, scrappy and able to go to ground after vermin, including the tough badger. Owners might find exploratory tunnels after a solo sojourn in the yard. Tracking ability, however, is all Scenthound. Despite their height, Dachshunds, even the Minis, are not wimpy pushovers. They're busy, inquisitive and active, and love to "help" rake leaves or keep the vacuum monster at bay. Dachsies like to know what people are doing, checking on them frequently, but independent enough to play with a toy in another room.

Overall, the Longhair tends to be the most docile. Smooths and Wires are often mischievous little scamps. With their family, Dachsies are comical and ready to play. Dachsies often favor one person, but Wires are more outgoing. These hounds can be con artists, wheedling an extra cookie or two or three. Owners are cautioned to watch their Dachsie's hourglass figure to prevent obesity from putting strain on weakened or damaged spinal supports.

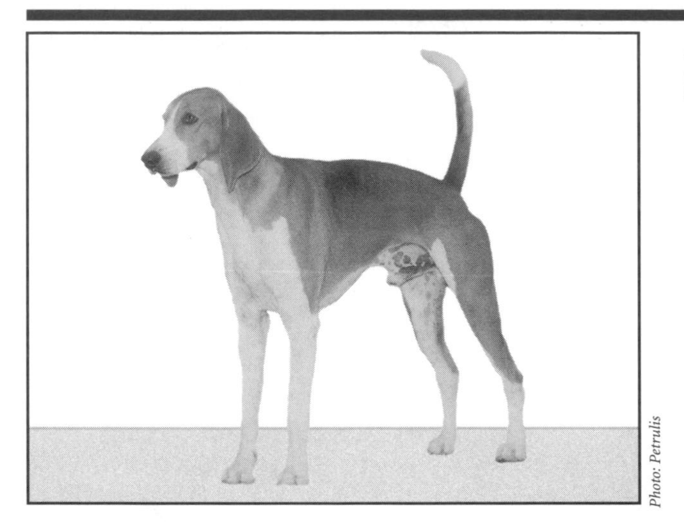

Photo: Petrulis

## American Foxhound

**Size:** Large, F. 21–24", M. 22–25"

**Color:** Any color

**Protection:** Will protect family

**Energy:** High

**Life expectancy:** 10–12 yrs.

**Children:** Loving and patient

**Other animals:** Social, enjoy another dog; studs can be growly in a one-on-one situation

**Abilities:** Fox hunting, Tracking, Field Trials

**Shedding/Grooming:** Yes / A weekly swipe with the brush

**Health clearances:** OFA; **Ask about:** HD, deafness, spinal degeneration, blood disorders

**Best with:** Exercise, fenced yards

***Not for:*** Homebound, inactive or frail owners

Foxhounds are amiable and do better with at least one other dog and plenty of people contact. Youngsters often learn to walk holding a Foxhound tail.

Foxhounds are fairly attentive, especially when concentrating on something they enjoy. The trick, therefore, is to convince them they want the same thing their owners do. The variable surface Tracking test and search and rescue are good outlets for their sniffing talents.

## English Foxhound

Photo: Ce Harrison-Wickline

**Size:** Large, 24–26", F. 60–80#; M. 75–95#

**Color:** Hound, black, tan and white

**Protection:** Low, but do bark

**Energy:** High, but not hyper

**Life expectancy:** 10+ yrs

**Children:** Yes; young dogs may be too exuberant for tots

**Other animals:** Enjoy a companion

**Abilities:** Fox hunting, Tracking

**Shedding/Grooming:** Minimal / Brush with soft brush or hound glove, wipe with damp towel

**Health clearances:** OFA, CERF; **Ask about:** HD, pancreatitis, renal disease

**Best with:** Secure fencing, patient, active people

***Not for:*** Toddlers, apartments, "invisible" fence, being alone, elderly, those incapable of dealing with strong dog

Foxhounds have been selected over generations to run tirelessly for hours. They must be confined when outdoors if owners want to have a dog for more than one day.

Foxhounds are amiable and often play, live or hunt in packs, but can accidentally injure toy breeds in rough play. As might be expected, they live in harmony with horses. The English Foxhounds are faster, but slightly shorter and heavier-boned than their American cousins.

## Greyhound

**Size:** Large, F. 60–65#; M. 65–70#

**Color:** Any color

**Protection:** Low, but will bark

**Energy:** Medium–high, lower in dogs over age of three

**Life expectancy:** 9–14 yrs.

**Children:** Patient and careful

**Other animals:** Submissive with other dogs, some males quarrelsome; small animals a temptation as prey

**Abilities:** Lure coursing, Agility, therapy

**Shedding/Grooming:** Minimal / Low maintenance

**Health clearances:** CERF; **Ask about:** PRA, bloat, hypothyroidism, bleeding disorders, esophageal problems, anesthesia sensitivity

**Best with:** Fenced yards, easygoing owners, runners, regular exercise

***Not for:*** Automatic Obedience, outdoor life, extreme temperatures, off-leash romps, loud, demanding people

The swiftest in dogdom, Greyhounds can outrun a horse on a sprint. They'll run you a merry race if they find themselves loose. Bred for short bursts of speed and amazing leaps rather than marathons, some work out with long-distance runners. Surprisingly, these hounds love to be couch potatoes, preferring soft bedding to the hard floor or cement kennel run. Greyhounds adapt well to small quarters, and even former racers adjust to condos or apartments with time. Owners should be aware these dogs can be escape artists.

They have a habit of jumping up and hugging people, disconcerting to a small child or a fragile person. The lean body belies a hearty appetite. Owners shouldn't leave a steak thawing on the counter unless they want to have peanut butter for supper. Greyhounds are the canine equivalent of pack rats, scavenging food, toys, blankets.

## Harrier

**Size:** Medium, M. 19–21", 45–60#; F. slightly smaller

**Color:** Any color

**Protection:** Low, but will bark

**Energy:** High

**Life expectancy:** 10–12 yrs.

**Children:** Yes, but enthusiastic in play

**Other animals:** Accept as part of pack, will chase small furry creatures

**Abilities:** Hunting, Tracking, Obedience, Agility

**Shedding/Grooming:** Low / Drip dry, use soft brush or hound glove

**Health clearances:** OFA, CERF; **Ask about:** HD, PRA, lens luxation, epilepsy

**Best with:** HIGH secure fences, active people, hunters, Obedience training

***Not for:*** Apartments, free roaming, impatient owners, lounge chair lizard

True to their group, howling and digging can be a problem. Harriers can be willful. Like little kids, they find it more fun to do their own thing. They retain the gentle playfulness, loving nature and enthusiasm of the Foxhounds.

Peasants hunted hare on foot with Harriers. These dogs are smaller and a bit more outgoing than Foxhounds. This is not a breed a buyer can find on a weekend. People must be prepared to search out breeders and wait. The Internet can be a good source. Adults are a good option if waiting for that rare litter becomes too frustrating.

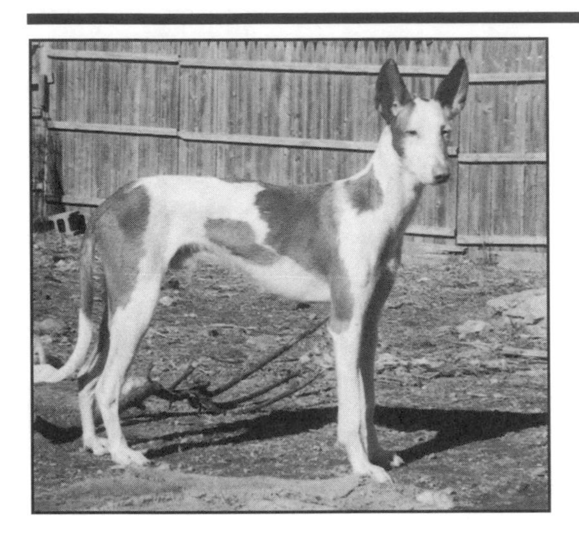

## Ibizan Hound

**Size:** Large, F. 22.5–26", 45#; M. 23.5–27.5", 50#

**Color:** White or red, solid or combination

**Protection:** Good watchdogs

**Energy:** Moderate–high

**Life expectancy:** 12–14 yrs.

**Children:** Excellent; may be too energetic for little ones

**Other animals:** Plays gently with even tiniest pets

**Abilities:** Lure coursing, hunting, Tracking, Obedience

**Shedding/Grooming:** Light / Weekly brushing

**Health clearances:** OFA, CERF; **Ask about:** Axonal dystrophy, cardiomyopathy, copper-associated hepatopathy

**Best with:** Exercise, a safe space to run and play

***Not for:*** Small apartments, elderly or invalids

This Gazehound was bred to hunt rabbits, and although not frequently the choice of hunters in Western civilization, care is taken not to lose instinct. The Ibizan's grace and sleek lines give a racy appearance, and swift they are. They show great stamina and tenacity. Secure play areas are important, as this breed can jump amazing heights.

As an uncommon breed, they're head turners. Their regal appearance is reminiscent of their homeland where it's believed the breed was the model for idols of Anubis.

## Irish Wolfhound

**Size:** Giant, F. 30"+, 105#; M. 32"+, 120#

**Color:** Gray, brindle, red, black, white, fawn

**Protection:** Size is intimidating, but not a guard dog

**Energy:** Low, unless they see a deer or rabbit

**Life expectancy:** 6 yrs.

**Children:** Calm and patient; size may be too much for tots

**Other animals:** Peaceable even with cats if not lure coursed

**Abilities:** Lure coursing

**Shedding/Grooming:** Minimal if groomed properly / Hand stripping, brushing

**Health clearances:** OFA, CERF; **Ask about:** vWD, EKG, HD, PRA, cataracts, bloat, cardiomyopathy, cancers (especially bone)

**Best with:** Owners who can handle size, fenced yard, lots of attention

***Not for:*** High-strung or extremely active people, jogging companion, guard dog, cubbyholes, harsh handling

The dignity of a diplomat, the power of a lion, the sensitivity of a priest, all describe the Wolfhound. The breed's heart is as big as its body. This gentle giant craves love and attention. It's a treat to watch this big beastie play gently with a toddler or a tiny Yorkie. Although rarely dominant, the breed tends to be stubborn.

Sadly, the Wolfhound's biggest drawback is the short lifespan. Buyers should look for lines with longevity. Owners should not allow puppies to jump or to stress fast-growing bones with strenuous exercise. High protein food, promoting rapid bone growth, is also to be avoided. Breeders recommend feeding twice a day and limiting exercise following meals to prevent bloat.

## Norwegian Elkhound

**Size:** Medium, F. 19.5", 35–48#; M. 20.5", 50–60#

**Color:** Gray

**Protection:** Good watchdog, fiercely loyal

**Energy:** High

**Life expectancy:** 10–12 yrs.

**Children:** Excellent, some might be too rambunctious with small ones

**Other animals:** Dominant, may quarrel with same sex; forget cats unless introduced in puppyhood

**Abilities:** Hunting, Tracking, sledding, herding

**Shedding/Grooming:** Perpetual, seasonally substantial / Pin and slicker brush weekly, use Greyhound comb

**Health clearances:** OFA, CERF; **Ask about:** HD*, PRA, cataracts, Fanconi's Syndrome, hypothyroidism

**Best with:** Fences; outdoorsy families; active social life; firm, fair owners who enjoy training a challenge

***Not for:*** Obedience enthusiasts; hair haters; frail, sedentary or submissive owners; those who want a silent dog

Closely related to Nordic breeds, Elkhounds have little in common with most Hounds other than their hunting ability. Their bold, energetic nature can lead them to dig, chase or escape. Elkies are not averse to voicing frustration or boredom (or alerting to a trespassing cat or bunny). Close neighbors might find a duo—or more—disturbing.

This breed is not a puppet on a string. They tend to stretch household rules as far as you'll let them, i.e., sleeping on the off-limits sofa at night. Elkies are wont to lie by forbidden territory, stretching out a foot onto the carpet, followed by a second foot, then a nose. Before owners know it, the dog is by their side. Elkhounds are chow hounds and can easily creep up to the chubbette size.

## Otterhound

Photo: K. Booth

**Size:** Large, F. 23–26", 65–100#; M. 24–27", 75–115#

**Color:** Usually black/tan, grizzle, red, liver/tan, tri or wheaten

**Protection:** Will sound alarm, territorial on home turf

**Energy:** Medium–high as youngsters, need regular exercise

**Life expectancy:** 12–14 yrs., late maturing

**Children:** Affectionate, like to romp and wrestle; happy tails can be hazardous to toddlers

**Other animals:** Enjoy working or playing with dogs; strange cats are in for a free-for-all

**Abilities:** Tracking, Agility, search and rescue, therapy

**Shedding/Grooming:** Seasonal, grooming helps / Weekly with slicker brush and comb, clean ears and beard frequently

**Health clearances:** OFA; **Ask about:** HD, bloat, seizures, bleeding disorders

**Best with:** Fences, hunters, outdoor folk, those who like sloppy kisses

***Not for:*** Jogging partners, fragile owners, off-lead walks, white carpeting, fastidious neatniks

This big, shaggy hound has a soft heart. Otterhounds adore water, their family and playing kissy-face with kids, not necessarily in that order. A puddle, pool or any body of water tempts this canine gold-medal swimmer. This is a breed that has no equal for underwater search and rescue.

OHs submerge their heads when drinking and come up shaking their beards. When used as hunting companions, they might track raccoons or big game. It's said, "When the nose turns on, the ears turn off." When on a scent, they give voice, described by owners as beautiful, possibly not so melodious to neighbors.

Owners describe some males as seeming "very grave and dignified and serious, almost surprising themselves when they do something playful or silly." One attraction is "a 120-pounder that thinks it's a lap dog." This is an uncommon breed, near the bottom in AKC numbers.

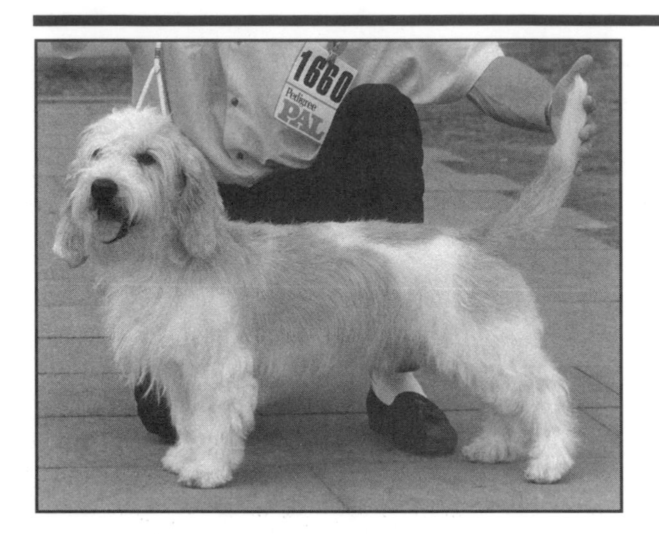


## Petit Basset Griffon Vendéen

**Size:** Small–medium, F. 12–14", 25–35#; M. 13–15", 30–45#

**Color:** White, with lemon, orange, black, tricolor or grizzle markings

**Protection:** Alert alarm dogs with a loud bass bark

**Energy:** High, M. may be less so; more moderate as adults

**Life expectancy:** 10–14 yrs.

**Children:** Excellent, can be too boisterous for young

**Other animals:** Play peacefully, but a bit bossy

**Abilities:** Hunting, Tracking, Agility, Field Trials

**Shedding/Grooming:** Minimal with weekly combing or brushing / Neaten tousled, whiskery appearance; pluck ear canal hair

**Health clearances:** OFA, CERF; **Ask about:** HD, patellar luxation, PRA, juvenile cataracts, epilepsy, juvenile meningitis, hypothyroidism

**Best with:** Long walks, fenced yard, socialization, outdoor exercise

***Not for:*** Snap-to Obedience, free roaming, sedentary owners, those who want a quiet pet

People who succumb to a fuzzy puppy face should be aware this is not just an adorable lap dog. PBGVs are bold, active, sturdy dogs with an urge to run after rabbits or to follow a enticing trail. Even with a fence, precautions must be taken to avoid a desire to dig and an amazing ability to jump. They like to bark, sometimes a problem in close quarters.

Males are often more biddable than females. PBGVs prefer to adjust to new surroundings or situations at their own speed. Their happy, playful clowning attracts owners who can chuckle at the mischievous streak.

## Pharaoh Hound

**Size:** Medium–large, F. 21–24"; M. 23–25"

**Color:** Tan to chestnut, with white markings

**Protection:** Observant and barks promptly

**Energy:** High, need two hours of exercise daily

**Life expectancy:** 11–15 yrs.

**Children:** Excellent, love to play

**Other animals:** Good

**Abilities:** Lure coursing, Obedience, Agility

**Shedding/Grooming:** Minimal / Brush or use hound glove

**Health clearances:** OFA, CERF; **Ask about:** Optic nerve hypoplasia

**Best with:** Exercise; fenced yard or leash walking and running a MUST

***Not for:*** Couch potatoes, heavy-handed owners

Any dog that accompanied Pharaohs on the hunt has 5,000 years of instinct urging it to hit the road when tempted. Their keen eyes can spot movement long before a person can. A furry critter can prove too great a temptation. They neither stop, look, nor listen. Disaster is certain if this dog is let off leash in an unprotected area. Sensible and cautious, Pharaohs prefer to set their own pace when introduced to new situations or people. Natural curiosity will urge the dog to check out the novelty.

When excited, Pharaohs have a quality unique in the canine world: They blush. A rosy glow colors nose, ears and even deepens the eyes. Occasionally, the Pharaohs' lips part in a smile and their eyes seem to look into history.

## Rhodesian Ridgeback

**Size:** Large, F. 24–26", 70#; M. 25–27", 85+#

**Color:** Light wheaten to red wheaten

**Protection:** High when there is a threat

**Energy:** High as youngsters

**Life expectancy:** 12 yrs.

**Children:** Gentle with toddlers, rough-and-tumble with older kids

**Other animals:** Threat to small ones unless raised with them

**Abilities:** Lure coursing, Tracking

**Shedding/Grooming:** Little / Brush weekly with stiff brush or curry comb

**Health clearances:** OFA; **Ask about:** HD, hypothyroidism, cancers, dermoid sinus

**Best with:** Fences; athletes; people with the ability to control a large, independent dog; early socialization and training

***Not for:*** Robot trainers; outside life, particularly in extreme cold

Intuitive Ridgebacks know when to use their extraordinary power. Lions are strong and fight savagely to avoid capture—and canines that track them are formidable opponents, sturdy and confident enough to control any situation. Owners of these canine lion tamers need to take the upper hand from the beginning.

A free spirit, this dog will test owners and push a point. Without respect and control, they can become bossy. They're dignified and aloof with strangers. Owners note a personality difference between the dogs with liver or black noses. The brown-nosed Ridgeback seems to enjoy playing the clown; the black-nosed strain is more dignified, with a drier wit. A strip of hair that grows like a cowlick up the back forms the ridge.

## Saluki

**Size:** Large, F. 21–23"; M. 24–26"

**Color:** A rainbow—white, cream, fawn, golden, red, grizzle and tan, tricolor, black and tan

**Protection:** Some alert to visitors (and birds or trucks)

**Energy:** High outside, low indoors

**Life expectancy:** 10–12 yrs.

**Children:** If raised with them, prefer older kids, dislike sudden or clumsy movement of toddlers

**Other animals:** Tolerates canines, but small creatures are considered prey

**Abilities:** Lure coursing, Obedience

**Shedding/Grooming:** Some / Brush tails and ears, use hound glove on rest

**Health clearances:** OFA, CERF; **Ask about:** HD, glaucoma, PRA, hypothyroidism, heart defects

**Best with:** Soft bedding, indoor living and fences a must, early socialization

***Not for:*** Small critters, someone who wants a clingy dog

Salukis demand respect and seem to sense their ancient history. They possess a regal air as if considering themselves more a companion than a pet. Fleet enough to capture a gazelle, Salukis retain hunting instinct and are liable to take off if tempted. Their slim, trim bodies are those of a well-tuned athlete.

When they choose, Salukis can be attentive. Otherwise, owners can prattle on to no avail, with words going in one fringed ear and out the other. The breed is reserved, not prone to frequent cuddling. Cat owners find the Saluki independence appealing. A snood keeps long ear hair from dangling in food and trailing crumbs.

## Scottish Deerhound

Photo: C. Brown

**Size:** Giant, F. 28+", 75–95#; M. 30–32+", 85–110#

**Color:** Dark blue-gray, gray, brindle, yellow and sandy red, red fawn

**Protection:** Nonexistent, view people as kind visitors

**Energy:** Quiet, calm, but must have running space

**Life expectancy:** 8–11 yrs.

**Children:** Excellent when socialized

**Other animals:** Fleet-footed felines turn on chase mode

**Abilities:** Lure coursing

**Shedding/Grooming:** Moderate / Minimal brushing and combing

**Health clearances:** OFA; **Ask about:** OCD, bloat, cardiomyopathy, osteosarcoma, toxin and anesthesia sensitivity

**Best with:** Athletes, large fenced spaces, woodsy areas for runs and "hunts," early socialization

***Not for:*** Oudoor life, guards, lap dogs, loud households, roughness

Deerhounds are as graceful as the animals they once hunted. Some may have to be encouraged to exercise. Yet when they break into a run, Deerhounds are poetry in motion. They might run for miles if owners have the facilities.

Their royal background comes through in their demeanor. With a regal bearing, they consider themselves at least equal to humans. As royalty, they don't fawn or pester for attention. A Deerhound can lie across the room and connect with owners through eyes and expression. Rarely used in the original capacity, the Deerhound is a charming, undemanding companion, one with dignity that doesn't feel it necessary to boast of blueblood ancestry.

## Whippet

**Size:** Medium, F. 18–21", 20–30#; M. 19–22", 25–40#

**Color:** Immaterial

**Protection:** None, but will bark to alert

**Energy:** Moderate

**Life expectancy:** 12–15 yrs.

**Children:** Excellent, but should go easy with roughhousing

**Other animals:** Happily accepted

**Abilities:** Lure coursing, straight or oval track racing

**Shedding/Grooming:** Minimal / Wash-and-wear, weekly brushing with hound glove

**Health clearances:** CERF, skin punch for SA; **Ask about:** PRA, cataracts, lens luxation, SA, heart defects

**Best with:** Fencing, secure space to run, the sports-minded

***Not for:*** Outdoor living, sedentary or heavy-handed owners, top Obedience competitors

Whippets' easygoing character and satin coat make them pleasant, loving companions and attuned to owners' moods. Whippets display moderation in all areas but one: flying after a lure when they're totally focused. Furry rodents or even a plastic bag blown across the yard might awaken the chase instinct. If such a temptation enters their eagle vision when in an unconfined area, the Whippet is gone in a flash, hitting speeds up to 35 miles an hour. This and their smaller appetites gave them the nickname of the "poor man's racehorse."

Their thin skin tends to tear easily from thorns, underbrush or other trauma. Tails are fragile. Low body fat demands coats or sweaters during cold weather outings. Soft bedding is recommended to cushion "bony" bodies. Winter often finds them snuggling in the owner's bed. Cat lovers are drawn to this clean, quiet dog that doesn't fawn or become obnoxious and is a pretty good mouser to boot.

# Working Breeds

5

# A Dog's Work Is Never Done (Working Breeds)

Without working canines, countries would remain unexplored, flocks would be vulnerable to attack, homes would be unprotected and soldiers would face battle alone. We'd have to carry our own loads. Even if we don't utilize a dog's working capabilities, chores pass more quickly when we have a four-footed buddy by our side.

As fits their profession, these dogs are all sturdy and strong, ready to pitch in and help when needed. An intruder with evil intent thinks twice about entering the premises guarded by one of this group. Loyal and protective, the guard dog boasts a bark that stops any heart mid-beat. Their demeanor speaks business, too. Bred to guard flocks, patrol estates, pull loads and sleds, aid fishermen and rescue people, some continue their duties today, still willing and capable. A parental swat could draw a growl of warning from toddlers' devoted guardians.

Their strength makes these dogs stalwart assistants for the physically challenged. Yet they are perfectly content lying on the hearth or back porch until needed. Those with Mastiff and flock guard roots require a minimal amount of exercise. Because they don't demand strenuous activity and are happy with a stroll around the backyard, they fit surprisingly well in small homes or even apartments. With all these attributes, many currently serve not only as assistance dogs, but in the military, police and search and rescue fields. The canine nose is ideal for scenting drugs or explosives.

The Nordic or sled dogs are actually a group unto themselves. Although they possess the working qualities needed to haul loads through the frigid northlands, they're more social, less territorial and free-spirited. Nordic breeds' owners say, "A loose dog is a lost dog."

The northern breeds are active and happier with a game of ball or other playtime. Ditto the Boxer, Standard Schnauzer and Portuguese Water Dog.

**General characteristics:** Alert, courageous, loyal, hardy, confident, territorial, protective, persistent, dominant. Take jobs seriously and are more content with work. Homebodies with the exception of the sled dogs, who MUST be confined.

Bark: good alarm dogs. Guard/Mastiff bark is booming bass. Sled dogs howl a distinctive "arooooo" and yak among themselves.

## Akita

Photo: J. C. photos

**Size:** Large, F. 24–26", 75–95#; M. 26–28", 85–115#

**Color:** Any color

**Protection:** Courageous, natural instinct to protect

**Energy:** Medium, calm house pets

**Life expectancy:** 10–12 yrs.

**Children:** Yes, with family; may be overprotective if playmates become rough

**Other animals:** Can be aggressive with dogs or small animals

**Abilities:** Tracking, Obedience, Weight Pulling, backpacking

**Shedding/Grooming:** Seasonal to year-round / Weekly pin brushing, use grooming rake

**Health clearances:** OFA, CERF, skin punch for SA; **Ask about:** HD, patellar luxation, PRA, hypothyroidism, vWD, bloat, SA, pemphigus, lupus, cancer

**Best with:** Six-foot fence, Obedience training, people contact, confident and experienced dog owners

***Not for:*** Attack training, ego boosters, meek or frail people

Bred to be independent and to track big game, Akitas needed to be stubborn and dominant. Akitas learn quickly once owners have gained their respect. They're not cuddlers and are often aloof to those outside their family. Although not fawning, they are loyal until their death.

Like most Working dogs, they're not prone to nervous pacing, pestering demands or needless barking. Their alert appearance and demeanor give owners a feeling of security.

## Alaskan Malamute

**Size:** Large, F. 23", 75#; M. 25", 85#

**Color:** Light gray to black with white markings; also all white

**Protection:** Low; very protective of food and territorial with other animals

**Energy:** Medium–low

**Life expectancy:** 10–12 yrs.

**Children:** Yes

**Other animals:** Can be aggressive until pack order is established

**Abilities:** Sledding, Weight Pulling, carting, backpacking

**Shedding/Grooming:** Heavy, seasonal / Weekly brushing

**Health clearances:** OFA, CERF; **Ask about:** HD, cataracts, chondrodysplasia, bloat, renal cortical hypoplasia, hypothyroidism, PDA, bleeding disorders

**Best with:** Fencing a must, exercise, protection from heat

***Not for:*** The easily intimidated, those unwilling or unable to control strong dog

Malamutes are workhorses and eagerly throw themselves into any activity. Malamutes are able—and happy—to pull loads many times their own weight. Food was scarce in the Arctic, and Mals still don't realize they don't have to protect or steal dinner. Anything edible within paw's reach is fair game. Owners should feed dogs separately to avoid confrontations.

Friendly and outgoing, Mals are sensitive to owners' moods, and sociable but not demanding. Although quiet companions, they talk to their owners in a captivating AROOOOO. Neighbors may find a chorus of these from several dogs less enchanting.

## Bernese Mountain Dog

**Size:** Large, 75–120#, F. 23–26"; M. 25–27.5"

**Color:** Tricolor (black with white and rust markings)

**Protection:** Low, will bark

**Energy:** Medium–low

**Life expectancy:** 8–10 yrs.

**Children:** Sweet and gentle, can knock down small children

**Other animals:** Social, enjoy company of another

**Abilities:** Draft, Agility, Obedience, Tracking

**Shedding/Grooming:** Bunches twice a year, other times minimal / Weekly brushing; regular ear cleaning

**Health clearances:** OFA hips and elbows, CERF; **Ask about:** HD*, elbow dysplasia, OCD, PRA, thyroid, histiocytosis, mast cell tumors, bloat, glomerulonephritis

**Best with:** Easygoing families, inclusion in most activities

***Not for:*** Seclusion, allergic or fastidious people

Berners happily join owners in work or play, eagerly pulling the kids in a wagon or bringing the cows home. Yet they're perfectly content to lie by owners' feet listening to Vivaldi or comforting during a late-night horror movie.

The Berner's size and happy tail can be fatal to coffee-table valuables. They're just the right size for a toddler to use for a boost and walking assistance. When little tykes take a tumble, tears are wiped away by Berner kisses. Breeders suggest feeding maintenance food to pups rather than high-growth puppy food.

## Boxer

**Size:** Medium–large, F. 21–23.5", 50–65#; M. 22.5–25", 65–80#

**Color:** Fawn or brindle, usually with white markings

**Protection:** Deep bark, size and looks may deter intruders

**Energy:** Exuberant but not hyperactive; mellows with age

**Life expectancy:** 8–12 yrs.

**Children:** "Outstanding"; protective, devoted babysitters, may be too exuberant for toddlers

**Other animals:** Harmonious, but males might struggle for dominance

**Abilities:** Obedience, therapy, Agility, service fields

**Shedding/Grooming:** Seasonal / Wash and-wear basics

**Health clearances:** OFA, CERF;
**Ask about:** HD, PRA, SAS, cardiomyopathy, torsion, epilepsy, bleeding disorders, cancerous tumors, colitis

**Best with:** Human contact, exercise, strong-minded owners

***Not for:*** The frail, people who want a docile pet, extremes of heat or cold

The Boxer's demand for attention may not suit people who prefer a more aloof pet. Although these dogs are strong and courageous enough to take on a foe, their happy wiggle gives them away for the softies they are. They'll adjust to a big family or one-person home life, being an "only" dog or one of many. Owners note that Boxers are clean and lick themselves like cats. The same dog that plays the clown with children and wriggles on the ground can turn into a noble, cleanly chiseled work of art at a mere command and the flick of a brush.

Breeders recommend care with diet, avoiding soy-based foods. Rich diets can cause digestive problems and the infamous flatulence. Their regrettably short lifespan is often caused by cancers, which breeders are working diligently to overcome. Drooling, so common with shortfaced dogs, has been considerably decreased.

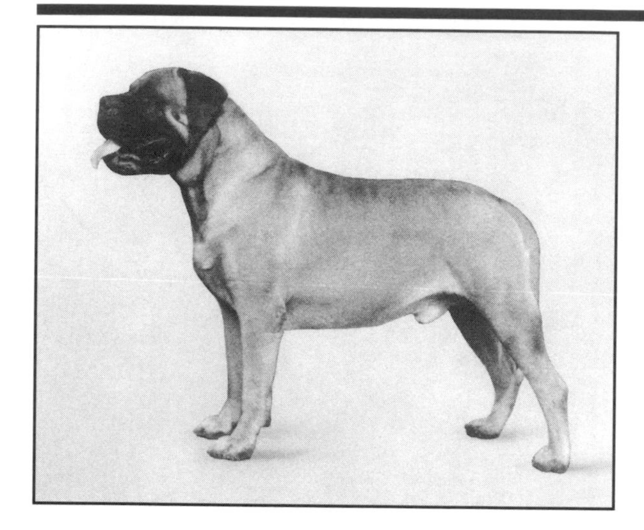

## Bullmastiff

**Size:** Large, F. 24–26", 100–120#; M. 25–27", 110–135#

**Color:** Red, fawn, brindle

**Protection:** Instinctively guard family and property

**Energy:** Low indoors, medium outdoors

**Life expectancy:** 10 yrs.

**Children:** Excellent when raised in family environment or socialized; can take guarding duties too seriously during rowdy play

**Other animals:** Accept and protect family pets; won't tolerate strangers trespassing; some same-sex challenges

**Abilities:** Obedience, Weight Pulling, Tracking, Agility

**Shedding/Grooming:** Seasonal / Brush to remove dead hair

**Health clearances:** OFA, CERF; **Ask about:** HD*, elbow dysplasia, PRA, ectropion, entropion, bloat/torsion

**Best with:** Fence, Obedience, socialization

***Not for:*** Attack, chaining, jogging companions, exercise in heat, frail or too-permissive people

The Bullmastiff was bred for short bursts of speed and the power to stop a poacher. Seldom required to enforce that duty today, they're undemanding companions and are content with less exercise than more streamlined breeds. Bullmastiffs relish physical contact, whether overflowing your lap or lying at (or on) your feet. Their strength lies in their brawn; they don't bark needlessly.

Bullmastiff Rescue recommends looking for the less dominant pup for families with children. Related to other "bull" and mastiff breeds, they are like Missourians: "Show me a reason for doing this, and I'll do it." But the best way to convince a Bullmastiff is to bond and foster mutual respect. What the breed won't do through orders or force, it will for love. Admittedly, bribes don't hurt. It's the rare human that can out-muscle a Bullmastiff!

## Doberman Pinscher

Photo: Shafer

**Size:** Large, 60–85#, F. 24–26"; M. 26–28"

**Color:** Black, red, blue or fawn, all with rust markings

**Protection:** High sense of territory

**Energy:** High

**Life expectancy:** 10–12 yrs.

**Children:** Affectionate; size might be overwhelming to small ones; may be overprotective

**Other animals:** Prefer to be alpha, but protective

**Abilities:** Tracking, Obedience, Flyball, Agility, service fields

**Shedding/Grooming:** Seasonal / Wash-and-wear

**Health clearances:** OFA, vWD; **Ask about:** HD, bloat, cancers, vWD, liver disease, hypothyroidism, geriatric spinal demyelinization

**Best with:** Indoor life, plenty of human interaction

***Not for:*** Easily dominated owners, those who don't want a dog that demands attention

The breed's sleek, well-muscled grace speaks of an aristocrat. Claimed the Cadillac protection dog, Dobies keep any intruder at bay. Yet they'll back off at a single command, alertly watching every move. They're totally fearless and will take on foes of any size. This breed often adopts an extended family, orphan kittens, other pets and neighbors.

Dobes are busy, always finding something that draws their attention. They're most content when given a job to do. Although bright, they are free thinkers and believe their way is best. Trainers must be able to control an animal that can be single-minded and possesses mental and physical strength.

## Giant Schnauzer

Photo: Linot

**Size:** Large, F. 23.5–25.5", 65–80#; M., 25.5–27.5", 80–95#

**Color:** Black or pepper-and-salt

**Protection:** Very high, take their job seriously

**Energy:** Medium–high, need two-mile walk and a game of catch

**Life expectancy:** 10–12 yrs.

**Children:** Tolerant and loving with their own, may be overprotective; show some herding instinct

**Other animals:** Dominant with others

**Abilities:** Tracking, Herding, Agility, Obedience, search and rescue, service fields

**Shedding/Grooming:** Low / Frequent brushing, stripping undercoat seasonally; comb beards daily

**Health clearances:** OFA, CERF; **Ask about:** HD*, OCD, PRA, glaucoma, heart defects, epilepsy

**Best with:** Exercise, Obedience training, fenced yard, time commitment, confident and firm owners

***Not for:*** Lazy groomers, first-time owners, those who want docile and quiet pets

Full of themselves, Giant Schnauzers like to be included in all activities. Many pet owners elect to have clipping and stripping done professionally.

"Owners can expect to be tested for top dog position." It requires mental domination to gain their respect. The size, dark color and exuberance of the Giant can be intimidating to a child and even some adults. Working breeds need a job to be content and to take their place in the family pack.

## Great Dane

Photo: Petrulis

**Size:** Giant, F. 32–34", 100–135#; M. 34–38", 145–185#

**Color:** Brindle, fawn, blue, black, harlequin (white with black patches)

**Protection:** High; size and bark alone are fearsome

**Energy:** Medium

**Life expectancy:** 8 yrs.

**Children:** Okay when raised with them; may be too much for tots

**Other animals:** Introduce early; some curl up with cats and dogs, others won't tolerate another four-footed creature on premises

**Abilities:** Obedience, Tracking, therapy, Agility

**Shedding/Grooming:** Some all year, heavier seasonally / Brush

**Health clearances:** OFA, CERF; **Ask about:** HD, HOD, cataracts, bone cancer, bloat, wobblers, deafness, enlarged heart

**Best with:** Early socialization and training, safe room for exercise, fenced yards, strong leadership

***Not for:*** Timid or very small children (or adults!), ignoring, tiny homes, puppy growth foods

Danes seem to know which way a busy owner is going to walk and sprawl in that path to gain attention. Happy Danes aren't always graceful and wagging tails can be injured or knock over valuables. When a pet grows to be bigger (and stronger) than the owner, aggression is dangerous. Discourage jumping on people. A Great Dane looking someone in the eyes can be intimidating! A Shih Tzu might chew a table leg, but a Dane can chomp the whole table.

The Dane eats like every meal is the last. Scooping the results of those meals takes a giant-size shovel. A trip to the vet necessitates a vehicle larger than the average Volkswagen bug. And they don't come in apartment size. Owning a BIG dog takes a big pocketbook and a heart to match.

## Great Pyrenees

**Size:** Giant, F. 25–29"; M. 27–32"

**Color:** White; may have gray badger, reddish brown or tan markings, especially on the head

**Protection:** High, barking may disturb neighbors; able to take on large, aggressive predators

**Energy:** Medium–low

**Life expectancy:** 10–12 yrs.

**Children:** Protective, patient and gentle

**Other animals:** Protective of family, drives off others

**Abilities:** Carting, backpacking, livestock guarding

**Shedding/Grooming:** Profuse / Brush weekly, comb or rake dead undercoat, trim eyebrows

**Health clearances:** OFA, CERF; **Ask about:** HD, elbow dysplasia, patellar luxation, cataracts, entropion, bleeding disorders, spinal problems, anesthesia sensitivity

**Best with:** Confinement, early training and socialization, kind firmness, consistent lifestyle

***Not for:*** Tying or chaining, small apartments or yards, competition Obedience, meek or frail owners unable to control giant strength and a strong-minded dog

The cuddly white cubs of Pyr pups quickly change as they reach full-grown bear size. These dogs are capable and willing to confront a perceived enemy—whether a burglar, a UPS driver or a sanitation worker. As flock guards, Pyrs might be totally on their own, making decisions and caring for themselves and their charges for a week or longer. Some lines and individuals have more working attributes, while others are better suited as family companions.

Their large-boned body and accompanying low metabolism means they are "easy keepers" on high-quality food. Sedate and dignified, Pyrs do anything for owners they respect. Pyrenees are calm house pets, never tearing from one room to the next or constantly underfoot.

## Greater Swiss Mountain Dog

**Size:** Giant, 90–130#, F. 23.5–27"; M 25.5–28"

**Color:** Black, rust, white

**Protection:** Protective of home turf

**Energy:** Medium

**Life expectancy:** 10 yrs

**Children:** Yes, much like the Bernese

**Other animals:** Accepts peacefully

**Abilities:** Weight Pulling, draft work, Obedience, Agility

**Shedding/Grooming:** Seasonal / Easy care, brush

**Health clearances:** OFA, CERF; **Ask about:** HD, elbow or shoulder dysplasia, OCD, bloat, torsion, hypothyroidism, splenic torsion, dilated esophagus

**Best with:** Family life, room to exercise

***Not for:*** Small confined areas, feeble owners, backyard mascots, jumping or rowdiness as youngsters

Much like its smaller cousin, the Bernese Mountain Dog, the Swissie was bred to assist the farmer and to pull heavy loads to market. After hours, children played with the Swissie and babies crawled unconcernedly over the easygoing dog as it played the role of nanny and protector.

Keeping them lean with controlled exercise helps keep Swissies in good health. To avoid stress on young bones, vigorous activities such as advanced Obedience, jogging or Weight Pulling should be put off until the Swissie is about two years old and mature. These are truly gentle giants, happiest when working, playing or just lounging around with their families.

## Komondor

**Size:** Large, F. 23.5+", 60#+; M. 25.5+", 80#+

**Color:** White

**Protection:** Very high; protect with heart, soul and powerful body

**Energy:** Basically calm house pets

**Life expectancy:** 12 yrs.

**Children:** With own family, can be overzealous in guarding

**Other animals:** Amiable with livestock and household pets

**Abilities:** Livestock guarding

**Shedding/Grooming:** Nearly nonexistent (knots into cords) / Time-consuming care starts at about eight months to separate cords; bathing takes about two hours, followed by 24 (YES!) hours' drying time

**Health clearances:** OFA, CERF; **Ask about:** HD, bloat, entropion, cataracts

**Best with:** Fenced yards, socialization and Obedience, fair but firm handling

***Not for:*** Ego boosters, lazy groomers, the meek or mild-mannered

The nearly non-shedding coat is a benefit for those with allergies. Another plus is the fact that Koms are easy keepers—many eat no more than three cups of dry food per day! Spur-of-the-moment purchases, however, often mean long-term regret or even rescue situations for the dog.

The coat is a magnet for more than dirt; it invites people to touch. Because Koms are naturally wary of strangers, socialization is a necessity from puppyhood. Unless precautions are taken, they're liable to mistake the mail carrier for a predator who daily threatens their flock. Despite their size, they can move quickly and, if one wishes to continue home deliveries, introductions and secure fencing are required. Pet situations demand a more mellow animal than a secluded flock guard. And, since pets are most often what is requested, responsible breeders screen buyers carefully and recommend Obedience classes.

## Kuvasz

**Size:** Giant, F. 26–28", 70–90#; M. 28–30", 100–115#

**Color:** White

**Protection:** Highly territorial, suspicious of strangers

**Energy:** Moderate–low, half an hour of play or walking

**Life expectancy:** 10 yrs.

**Children:** If raised with them, can be protective

**Other animals:** Good with household pets; challenges others

**Abilities:** Livestock guard, Tracking, Obedience

**Shedding/Grooming:** Constantly, heavy seasonal / Brush weekly

**Health clearances:** OFA, CERF; **Ask about:** vWD; HD*, elbow dysplasia, OCD, deafness, torsion, hypothyroidism, blood disorders

**Best with:** Confident owners, fenced yard, early and continuing socialization and Obedience

***Not for:*** Novice owners, neatniks, open-door policy, inactive people, small apartments

The Kuvasz has a highly developed parental instinct, causing it to "adopt" orphaned lambs, kittens or other animals. Protective instincts are not always discerning. A scuffle between children could be perceived as a threatening situation. With a large, assertive dog, barking can be a problem unless owners develop a method of stopping it.

A one-family dog, the Kuvasz is often most attached to one person, and is sensitive to loud voices. The more the dog is included in family life, the more likely it is to protect its own, yet accept guests. The dog is said to "be loyal to friends and never forgets enemies."

## Mastiff

**Size:** Giant, F. 120–165#; M. 165–225# (pets often 10–40# smaller)

**Color:** Fawn, apricot or brindle

**Protection:** Deterrent due to size and appearance; not barkers; some lines more aggressive

**Energy:** Mellow, quiet and calm

**Life expectancy:** 5–10 yrs.

**Children:** Some lines better than others; socialize

**Other animals:** Peaceful; may allow others to dominate

**Abilities:** Weight Pulling, Tracking, therapy, Obedience

**Shedding/Grooming:** Constant, but not profuse / Use shedding blade; "clean eye goobers and wipe jowls five to twenty times daily"

**Health clearances:** OFA, CERF; **Ask about:** vWD, HD*, elbow dysplasia, OCD, HOD, patellar luxation, eye defects, hypothyroidism, cardiomyopathy, strokes, bloat, epilepsy, spondylosis

**Best with:** Careful purchase; financial resources to cover vet care, a large automobile and a giant appetite

***Not for:*** Small apartments, neatniks, lazy trainers, kennel dogs

Extremely laid back, Mastiffs are happy watching owners complete chores. If invited, however, they join in activities, dancing and singing at the sight of leashes. Scrubbing walls and floors is part of a Mastiff owner's life. Big feet track in dirt. A shake can fling drool across the room. Breeders advise feeding with a natural low protein, low fat food.

Their nobility and courage impresses both friend and foe. It's important to socialize, however, and to research a purchase to find these easygoing beasties. Dominant and dog-aggressive lines can be problems for novice owners. Ideal temperament is soft, sweet and trainable.

## Newfoundland

**Size:** Giant, 28–32", 120–150#

**Color:** Black, Landseer (black and white), bronze and blue

**Protection:** Medium, has a "thundering" bark, size elicits respect, "possesses courage without ferocity"

**Energy:** Medium–low at maturity

**Life expectancy:** 10 yrs.

**Children:** Prefers children to adults!

**Other animals:** Usually sociable

**Abilities:** Water rescue, draft work, therapy, Obedience, Tracking, backpacking

**Shedding/Grooming:** Yes, bags full! / Weekly combing and brushing with slicker brush, more frequently in summer

**Health clearances:** OFA, heart clearance; **Ask about:** HD*, OCD, bloat, SAS, entropion, ectropion, hypothyroidism

**Best with:** Kids, exercise, manners

***Not for:*** Apartments, the houseproud, extreme high temperatures, overfeeding

Described as benevolent and dignified when mature, Newfs are good family pets. Buyers should realize, however, the cuddly little panda or bear cub quickly grows into a giant, hulking dog that drools and sheds. Breeders advise buyers not to roughhouse or wrestle with the puppy because the grown dogs are not aware of their size.

Newfies often accompanied and assisted sailors as well as rescuing drowning victims. They are sometimes overzealous in their career. Swimmers, especially children, occasionally find themselves towed repeatedly to the edge of a pool by an anxious canine lifeguard. They are powerful swimmers and relish all water work. On land, they enjoy pulling the kids around in a cart, pulling a sledge with firewood or backpacking with a buddy.

## Portuguese Water Dog

**Size:** Medium, F. 17–21", 34–50#; M. 19–23", 42–60#

**Color:** Black, white, brown, particolor

**Protection:** Medium–high

**Energy:** High

**Life expectancy:** 10–14 yrs.

**Children:** Yes, but treat kids as peers rather than obeying them; sometimes herd or tackle in exuberant play

**Other animals:** Relate well, can be jealous or territorial

**Abilities:** Obedience, Agility, water work, herding

**Shedding/Grooming:** Minimal, good for allergic people / Maximum daily brushing and combing, scissoring or clipping monthly

**Health clearances:** OFA, CERF, GM-1 N; **Ask about:** HD, PRA, GM-1 (glycogen storage disease)

**Best with:** Playing games, frequent grooming, active and social people

***Not for:*** Ignoring, harsh corrections, sofa decoration

Porties are bouncy, versatile and fuzzy-wuzzy. Yet problems arise when buyers believe this cuddly pup is going to grow up into a bigger, decorative teddy bear. These dogs want to work and play, preferably with their owners. If not, an owner might have to buy the Portie a pet to release the breed's energy and play drive. Like a human infant, Porties investigate things by putting them into their mouths. A sock or wallet left on the floor is not long for this world.

Porties often choose a cool surface to lie on. Owners may find them snoozing in a bathtub. These dogs happily dive into the coldest water. People joke that it's possible, with the industriousness of the breed, Porties swam from Portugal to America!

## Rottweiler

Photo: W. Cook

**Size:** Large, F 22–25", 80–100#; M. 24–27", 95–135#

**Color:** Black, with rust to mahogany markings

**Protection:** Highly territorial

**Energy:** Medium

**Life expectancy:** 8–9 yrs.

**Children:** Depends on individual; school age better match for size of dog; may show latent herding instinct by bumping and shouldering

**Other animals:** Expose early on, some same-sex aggression

**Abilities:** Herding, Weight Pulling, carting, Tracking, Obedience, service fields

**Shedding/Grooming:** Yes, yes, yes / Minimal, brush

**Health clearances:** OFA, CERF, heart exam; **Ask about:** HD*, elbow dysplasia, OCD, PRA and other retinal problems, heart defects, cancer, bloat, hypothyroidism

**Best with:** Early, continuous Obedience and socialization; fences; firm, fair, consistent discipline; strong, confident owners

***Not for:*** Pushovers, chaining or tying, invisible fences, elderly or infirm, status symbol, first-time owners

The American Rottweiler Club states, "The Rottweiler is an eager partner but a reluctant slave." They're simply too strong and determined to be forced. What Rotties do is done for an owner they love and respect. Control of a powerful dog is a necessity, not a nicety. An out-of-control Siberian or Basset might dig, howl, run off or be obnoxious with guests, but with a powerful guarding breed, consequences can be much more serious.

Calm and confident, the breed's courage is legendary. Loving to their own family, these dogs are aloof with strangers and need to be introduced to visitors, veterinarians and others met in life. They can't be expected to discern between shouts of anger and whoops of delight; between a threatening shove and football tackles; or the sneakiness of someone intending violence or playing hide-and-go-seek. Avoid dominance games such as tug-of-war.

## Saint Bernard

Photo: Booth

**Size:** Giant, F. 25–30", M. 27–34"

**Color:** Red and white

**Protection:** Size and bark deter strangers; naturally protective

**Energy:** Medium–low; short bursts of energy, especially as puppies

**Life expectancy:** 8 yrs.

**Children:** Socialize early; research bloodlines

**Other animals:** Co-exist in peace when raised with them

**Abilities:** Draft work, Weight Pulling, search and rescue

**Shedding/Grooming:** Seasonal / Weekly brushing; longhaired variety needs a bit more brushing than shorthaired

**Health clearances:** OFA; **Ask about:** HD*, OCD, bloat, cancer, epilepsy, entropion, ectropion, heart problems

**Best with:** Cool facilities; confident, strong owners

***Not for:*** Invalids, elderly, tidy housekeepers, weak-willed people, hot and humid weather

Saints were bred to serve humans, and they'll happily do many chores, hauling anything from a load of logs to a wagon with kids. They're more willing to serve when there's mutual respect between canine and master. Mr. America couldn't budge a determined Saint, but Miss America could convince it with affection and a bit of dog psychology. To live peacefully with a Saint, it's recommended that owners must control protection instincts rather than encourage them. Due to sheer size, Saints often retain the alpha role among other pets without challenge. One Saint allows her tiny kennel mates, Norwich Terriers, to run up and down her back.

With a high incidence of hip dysplasia in the breed, it is necessary to choose wisely. A crippled Saint is often a dead Saint because of the weight on the joints causing pain. Owners simply can't carry them. Large jowls mean drooling is a fact of life. Pet buyers, especially, prefer tighter lips and a dry mouth.

## Samoyed

**Size:** Medium, F. 19–21", 38–50#; M. 21–24", 50–65#

**Color:** White (can have cream or biscuit spots, especially on head)

**Protection:** Will bark, otherwise NONE!—they love everyone

**Energy:** Medium, eager to join in games

**Life expectancy:** 12–15 yrs.

**Children:** Excellent, especially when raised with them

**Other animals:** Usually friendly

**Abilities:** Herding, dog sledding, Obedience, Weight Pulling, hiking, therapy

**Shedding/Grooming:** F. seasonal, M. once a year / Brushing (though less than one would think), bikini and foot pad trim

**Health clearances:** OFA, CERF; **Ask about:** HD, PRA, cataracts, hypothyroidism, diabetes

**Best with:** Cold-weather sports, daily exercise, fenced yards, patience, emotional commitment

***Not for:*** Control freaks, warm humid climates, backyard dog, frail people, wearers of dark clothing!

There's more to this dog than a Vogue face and hair. A canine Will Rogers, Samoyeds have never met a person they don't like. Or almost any other animal. Sams stay puppy-waggy throughout life and are the original party animals. Much like toddlers, a Sam puppy will test your patience, then befog your brain with kisses and adorable "Who, me?" looks. Owners state, "True Sams have about two and a half retrieves in them," thinking if you throw it away you must not want it. With a history of herding reindeer, they'll easily transfer that drive to livestock.

Samoyeds are easy keepers. Many are on owner-imposed diets. The Sammy smile is a hallmark of the breed and is called for in the Standard.

## Siberian Husky

**Size:** Medium, F. 20–21"; M. 21–23.5"

**Color:** All colors from black to white, usually with markings

**Protection:** Will bark

**Energy:** Moderately high

**Life expectancy:** 12–14 yrs.

**Children:** Yes, good in a secure area

**Other animals:** Social, enjoy canine companionship; cannot be trusted with farm animals or small domestic pets—cats and Siberians in same house means flying fur

**Abilities:** Dog sledding, backpacking, hiking, ski-joring

**Shedding/Grooming:** Seasonal, profuse / Brush frequently; comb during shed

**Health clearances:** OFA, CERF; **Ask about:** HD, PRA, cataracts, corneal dystrophy, glaucoma

**Best with:** Active, outdoor lovers; fenced yard a must; firm-minded owners

***Not for:*** Protection, isolation, off-leash walks

Siberians were bred to run and for speed. If the urge hits them to take off, it's impossible to catch them on foot. And unlike many dogs, Siberians are not likely to return home when they finally stop. Digging can prove a problem for the bored Siberian.

Their free spirit, enthusiasm and stamina appeal to athletes. Not all owners have the opportunity or desire to "mush," but Siberians will happily pull a youngster in a wagon or a sled. They're also great buddies for cross-country skiing or ski-joring, a sport in which the dog is harnessed to the skier.

## Standard Schnauzer

**Size:** Medium, around 45#. F. 17.5–18.5"; M. 18.5–19.5"

**Color:** Pepper and salt, or black

**Protection:** Strong territorial instincts; will stand ground, but not aggressive

**Energy:** High

**Life expectancy:** 12–14 yrs.

**Children:** Tolerant, playful, rarely first to quit in game

**Other animals:** Alpha, but accepting; expose early

**Abilities:** Obedience, Agility, Tracking, service fields, search and rescue

**Shedding/Grooming:** Very little when properly groomed / Brush, hand strip and trim

**Health clearances:** OFA, CERF; **Ask about:** HD, hypothyroidism, cataracts, cancer

**Best with:** Active, confident owners; fenced yard; lots of exercise, training, and socialization

***Not for:*** Fireside companions, mild-mannered pushovers, those unwilling to care for grooming needs

As a puppy, the Standard Schnauzer "seems to explode with vim, vigor and relentless energy." Although they slow from jet propulsion to a trot as they mature, Standards remain active into their teen years. Described as "the dog with a human brain," the Standard Schnauzer enjoys problem solving (or what they perceive as problems, i.e., boredom) and will find a solution to nearly any dilemma. They're persistent and diligent and, like cats, stay on duty for hours if necessary.

Socialization and planned activities utilize this potential in a positive manner. It's much better to plan a nightly run and weekly Agility course than to fill in the forty-foot mole excavation.

# Terriers

# 6 Heart of a Lion (Terriers)

Although these dogs strike terror into the hearts of mice, rats and other vermin, the name "terrier" wasn't derived from "terror," but rather from *terra,* or earth. Because many small rodents live or hide in the ground, terriers are said to "go to ground" after their prey.

And they go after these pests with gusto. Little wonder so many farm homes raised Rat Terriers along with other animals. Even the smallest of this group have mighty hearts. Their confidence is liable to cause trouble when they confront a much larger (perceived) enemy. They don't give up and won't back down from a challenge, facing up to foxes, badgers and weasels. It's not unusual even for one of the small Terriers to protectively bark a warning from an owner's arms or at your ankles when you enter. Because of their fearless attitude, they make good watchdogs.

These scrappy dogs fended for themselves at a time when owners had trouble feeding children, let alone a dog. Today they're admired for their spunk and resilience. Even the smallest Terriers have a proud carriage and cocky attitude. Pets are sometimes clipped instead of hand stripped, but this does change the texture and color of coat.

Terriers are appealing to owners who want a sturdy, fearless dog without much bulk. Usually playful and outgoing with people, they may spar with other dogs. Busy and curious, terriers do not demand constant attention. They're good companions for people who live alone, as they'll sound an alert at the approach of every menacing squirrel. Terriers walk briskly and always find something of interest to investigate.

Prey instinct can be tested in Terrier Trials. Earth Tests are held by several clubs. Wooden tunnels are buried in the ground or under dirt mounds. Tunnels can also be created by bales of hay. Spirited terriers dart through underground burrows to caged prey or an enticing scent. As if gnashing teeth weren't enough to intimidate their opponents, they bark warnings as well.

**General characteristics:** Feisty, confident, busy, curious, courageous, tenacious, dominant. Many retain strong prey instinct.

Bark: sharp, staccato warning; love to hear their own voices.

## Airedale Terrier

Photo: K. Booth

**Size:** Medium–large, 45–70#, M. 23"; F. slightly less

**Color:** Black and tan

**Protection:** Warning bark, can back it up

**Energy:** High

**Life expectancy:** 10–13 yrs.

**Children:** With early exposure and socialization; may play too rough for small ones

**Other animals:** Mixes well if exposed early

**Abilities:** Obedience, Tracking, search and rescue, hunting small game, therapy, Agility, service

**Shedding/Grooming:** Minimal / Hand stripping for show, clipping for pets

**Health clearances:** OFA; **Ask about:** vWD, hypothyroidism, bleeding disorders

**Best with:** Owner interaction, outdoor sports, commitment to grooming and training, active people who are strong mentally and physically

***Not for:*** Timid or frail people, control freaks, heavy-handed corrections

When owners are busy with chores, Airedales can entertain themselves or take a catnap. Breeders say, "The Airedale has a sense of humor and an independent spirit that requires courting as a partner to get the full potential out of these dogs. They will not be bullied, do not suffer fools gladly and will neither fawn nor grovel. If you allow their dignity and accord them a sense of self, there is nothing the breed won't do for you."

This dog was bred to be the stalwart foe of badgers and is tough enough to hang on to snarling quarry. They are better convinced than coerced. Fanciers warn that the toughness of the beast makes them stoic. Owners must be in tune to their animals to be aware of illness or injury. Airedales needs to learn their place in the "pack" through firm consistent handling by all family members.

## American Staffordshire Terrier

**Size:** Medium, 40–75#, F. 17–18"; M. 18–19"

**Color:** Almost any solid, parti- or brindled colors

**Protection:** Medium–high

**Energy:** Medium–high

**Life expectancy:** 10–12 yrs.

**Children:** Usually trustworthy and tolerant; may be too exuberant for little ones

**Other animals:** Need to be supervised

**Abilities:** Obedience, Agility, Tracking, Flyball, carting, Weight Pulling

**Shedding/Grooming:** Some / Easy care, brush with rubber curry comb

**Health clearances:** OFA, CERF; **Ask about:** CMO, cataracts, hypothyroidism, cruiciate ligament ruptures, cancers

**Best with:** Activity, secure fences, close bonding, early training and socialization

***Not for:*** Aggression, ignoring, impatient trainers, ego boosters, macho image

Not as barky as many terriers, the AmStaff is deemed an excellent judge of character. The same dog that rolls around the floor with kids and greets your mother with a wag is willing and able to back a husky intruder out the door. They can be escape artists, opening gates or climbing, jumping or digging to freedom. A loose AST can be a dead dog because they fit the public's concept of "Pit Bull," and are deemed a threat. In several areas, bull breeds (including AmStaffs, Bull Terriers, Staffordshire Bull Terriers and others), sadly, have been banned. Muzzling or other legal restrictions may apply. Care must be taken to demonstrate responsibility to avoid discrimination.

A well-bred AmStaff is loving and playful, happy to snuggle, play the clown or jog by your side. Owners call them "Velcro dogs," because they stick close to you. Like most terriers, ASTs do have their own mind, and owners should stay one step ahead of them to out-think their pets. It's said puppies "chew with great gusto" and should be supplied with tough, resilient toys. They have strong jaws, and a coffee table can quickly be turned into toothpicks. Mouthing humans is a no-no and must be "nipped" in the bud.

## Australian Terrier

**Size:** Small, 10–11", 14–18#

**Color:** Sandy, red, or blue and tan

**Protection:** Amazingly deep barks

**Energy:** Medium–high as puppies, more settled later

**Life expectancy:** 12–15 yrs.

**Children:** Yes, if raised with them

**Other animals:** Enjoy a romp, better with opposite sex

**Abilities:** Agility, Tracking, Earthdog Tests, Obedience

**Shedding/Grooming:** Minimal, if properly groomed / Brush and comb 2–3 times weekly; trim furnishings monthly

**Health clearances:** OFA; **Ask about:** Legg-Perthes, patellar luxation, diabetes

**Best with:** Fence or walks on leash; fair, consistent discipline

***Not for:*** Soft-hearted pushovers, allergic people, outdoor living

Despite their size, Aussies are willing to take on foes of any size, mouse or moose, snail or snake. Given the chance, these little Terriers chase rodents and other small animals and can find themselves in trouble or far from home. Although they'll use their bark to sound an alarm, they're more easily quieted than many of their group. Described as "laid back for a terrier," they still need to be taught their place. Otherwise, the Aussie will be the one lying by the fire, while his owners fetch and carry.

Not a toy or decoration, the Australian Terrier was bred to be a worker. Owners can be confident Aussies will stand watch over their turf, yet be sensible enough to follow direction and small enough to control.

## Bedlington Terrier

**Size:** Medium, around 20#, F. 15–16.5"; M. 16–17.5"

**Color:** Blue, sandy or liver, with or without tan markings

**Protection:** Medium, will bark but seldom bite

**Energy:** Medium; enjoys playing, but calm house pet

**Life expectancy:** 15–16 yrs.

**Children:** Yes, especially if exposed early

**Other animals:** Accepts other pets

**Abilities:** Obedience, Agility, Tracking

**Shedding/Grooming:** Nearly none / Weekly combing, hand scissoring every two months; most pets professionally groomed

**Health clearances:** OFA, CERF; **Ask about:** Liver biopsy, copper toxicosis, cataracts, patellar luxation

**Best with:** Cuddlers, easygoing people, those who enjoy "coiffing"

***Not for:*** Outdoor living, lazy groomers, harsh corrections

The unique lamblike appearance and sweet temperament of the Bedlington sparks interest. Admirers enjoy a tractable pet focused on his owner. It's hard to resist snuggling with the stuffed-animal plushness of the breed. This terrier is an amiable dog, though sometimes reserved with strangers. "Squeaky rodents are at risk." Bedlingtons are elegant and whimsical, drawing attention wherever they go.

## Border Terrier

**Size:** Small, F. 11.5–14", 12–16#; M. 12–15.5", 12–20#

**Color:** Red, grizzle and tan, blue and tan, wheaten

**Protection:** Will bark an alarm

**Energy:** Moderately high

**Life expectancy:** 12–15+ yrs.

**Children:** Playful, tolerant, sturdy; may be too rough for tots

**Other animals:** Play well if raised with them; rabbits and stray cats deemed prey

**Abilities:** Earthdog Tests, hunting, Tracking, Agility, Flyball, therapy, Obedience

**Shedding/Grooming:** Minimal to moderate with regular grooming / Weekly slicker brushing, hand strip every six months

**Health clearances:** OFA, CERF; **Ask about:** Legg-Perthes, patellar luxation, cataracts, autoimmune problems, hypothyroidism, heart murmurs, seizures

**Best with:** Romps, long walks, secure fenced yards, early training, plenty of chew toys, lots of interaction

***Not for:*** Glamour pet, backyard dog, free feeding, perfect Obedience scores

The Border Terrier can be a pillow pal or a mountain climber. Ready to join in any children's game, these dogs will also sit in a bookworm's lap. These compact, whiskery pups have terrier stamina, intelligence, playfulness and ratting instinct, without the dominance, aggression, barking, coat care, or high energy of many in their group. They like to follow their people around, yet they're content to lie near them rather than being a "nudge."

Running loose is many a Border's downfall. The squirrel or kids across the street can tempt them into the path of a car. Their small packaging and determination mean they can work their way through brush or a rotting board. Borders are chow hounds and blimp out if given a chance. Neglecting the coat turns them into little brown "bushes" that profusely shed bristly hair, which works into upholstery. Buyers must find a good breeder, then be prepared to wait.

## Bull Terrier

**Size:** Medium, 30–65#

**Color:** White; colored BT may be brindle or any color

**Protection:** Medium–high, will bark

**Energy:** High

**Life expectancy:** 11–14 yrs.

**Children:** Generally very good; socialize early

**Other animals:** Some friendly with family pets, others can be quarrelsome

**Abilities:** Flyball, Agility, Weight Pulling

**Shedding/Grooming:** Minimal when brushed / Brushing

**Health clearances:** OFA, BAER, urinalysis; **Ask about:** Patellar luxation, lens luxation, heart defects, deafness, renal cortical hypoplasia

**Best with:** Regular training, exercise, sense of humor, a firm fair hand, lots of chew toys

***Not for:*** Outdoor living, pushovers, running loose

Bull Terriers love to be the center of attention and can be the ringmaster of their own circus. Prone to "Bully runs," they have high bursts of energy, tearing through the house, bouncing off furniture and skidding around corners. It's not funny, however, to come home to furniture that has been chewed into kindling. Their powerful jaws can destroy a family heirloom in minutes.

Bullies like to be up close and personal with their owners, sitting on laps, helping with household chores, guarding against the vacuum monster. The powerful, muscular body and strong, independent intellect mean the Bully can't be coerced. Persuasion by a respected and loved owner is the key to a happy household.

## Cairn Terrier

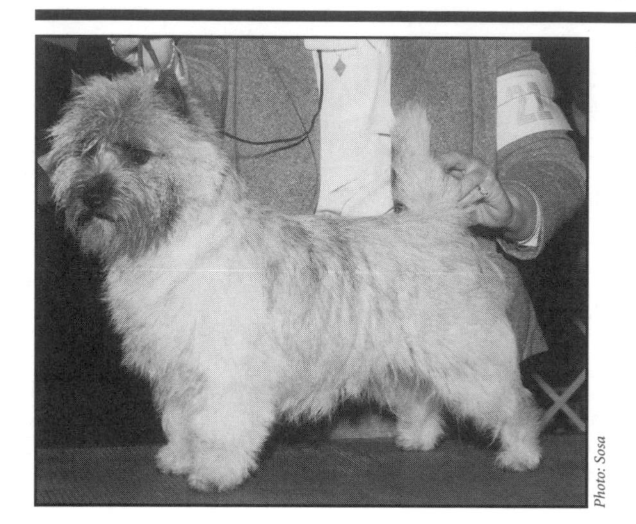

*Photo: Sosa*

**Size:** Small, F. 9.5", 13#; M. 10–12", 14–16#

**Color:** Any color except white

**Protection:** Definitely will bark

**Energy:** High, but not high-strung

**Life expectancy:** 14–16 yrs.

**Children:** Very good, vigorous playmate

**Other animals:** Endeavor to be Top Dog

**Abilities:** Terrier Trials, Tracking, Agility

**Shedding/Grooming:** Seasonal / Brush and comb; hand strip for show (annually for pets, or trim with thinning shears)

**Health clearances:** OFA, CERF; **Ask about:** vWD, Legg-Perthes, patellar luxation, CMO, PRA, cataracts, glaucoma, blood disorders, kidney problems

**Best with:** Fence, alpha owners

***Not for:*** Silence; co-existence with small pets; instant, constant Obedience

The Cairn's bustling inquisitiveness means owners are never lonely when he's around. He learns quickly, but makes up his own mind whether to listen or investigate an intriguing hole. A secure area is a necessity, or owners may find their resourceful pet happily barking at a treed squirrel after tunneling under the fence. This friendly little dog is always happy to see people and will bark to share his joy with the world. They'll also spread the word when a rabbit, cat or other critter enters the area.

The Cairn Terrier Club of America is one of the frontrunners in attacking health problems, encouraging testing and maintaining an open registry of tested dogs. None of the problems found within the breed is listed as common. Rather, they are infrequent, and conscientious breeders work to decrease or eradicate that percentage.

## Dandie Dinmont Terrier

Photo: Kernan

**Size:** Medium–small, 8–11", 18–24#

**Color:** Pepper or mustard

**Protection:** Very protective

**Energy:** Moderately high

**Life expectancy:** 13–15 yrs

**Children:** Usually; expose early

**Other animals:** When raised with them

**Abilities:** Obedience, Tracking, Terrier Trials

**Shedding/Grooming:** Minimal if groomed properly / Brushing, combing, hand stripping

**Health clearances:** OFA, CERF; **Ask about:** Elbow deformity, patellar/shoulder luxation, glaucoma, hypothyroidism, Intervertebral disk disease

**Best with:** Fenced yards, confident owners

***Not for:*** Lazy groomers, weak-willed people

Contrary to the name, Dandies are rough-and-tumble, tenacious and go-getters, especially when it's something they want. Determined and confident, the Dandie is a good companion for someone who wants an assured dog that is happy and affectionate, but doesn't fawn. The Dandie is more reserved than many terriers. Their hearts are won, not given wantonly.

Dandies stand their ground if pushed, and take on the toughest underground varmint with ease. Dandies' size and mentality allow them to fit happily almost anywhere: apartment or condo, Corvette or Jeep.

Photo: K. Booth

## Smooth Fox Terrier

**Size:** Medium, F. 14–16", 15–20#; M. 15–17", 20–25#

**Color:** Mostly white with black and/or tan markings

**Protection:** Alert and territorial, will set off an alarm

**Energy:** Loves to go-go-go; some may mellow with time

**Life expectancy:** 12–14 yrs.

**Children:** Best for active children six or older

**Other animals:** Larger dogs respected; challenge same size and sex

**Abilities:** Obedience, Agility, Terrier races, Earthdog Tests, hunting small game

**Shedding/Grooming:** Seasonal shed of white, spiky hair that sticks to everything / Brushing

**Health clearances:** OFA, CERF; **Ask about:** Legg-Perthes, PRA, cataracts, heart problems, epilepsy

**Best with:** Active owners, training, fences, hikers, small-game hunters, firm and patient training, experienced owners

***Not for:*** Robotic Obedience, backyard dogs, the elderly or sedentary, multiple-dog households

The cheerful Fox Terriers think the world was made for them. With sufficient exercise, this breed can be happy in a small apartment. Fox Terriers love toys and entertain themselves for hours. If bored, they can become escape artists, digging, jumping or squeezing through an opening to freedom. They're fearless and daring, which is their downfall if they're allowed to rule the home turf or run loose.

Give them a varmint to watch, and they'll stand guard for hours. They will tolerate cats (or at least give them regular exercise) if raised with them, but forget gerbils, hamsters and other creepy-crawlies. They're eager hunting companions for small game and will take on a 30-pound fox. One of the breed's best attributes is being "companionable without being clinging."

## Wire Fox Terrier

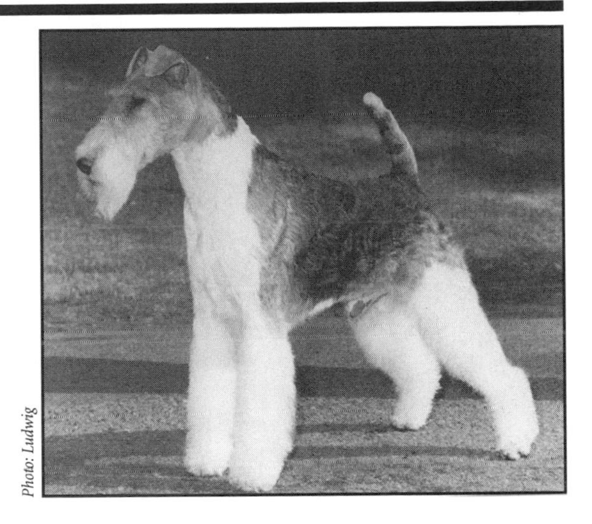
Photo: Ludwig

**Size:** Medium, F. 14–16", 15–20#; M. 15–17", 20–25#; show no more than 15.5", 18#

**Color:** Mostly white with black and/or tan markings

**Protection:** Alert, with big-dog bark

**Energy:** High, mellows with time

**Life expectancy:** 12–14 yrs.

**Children:** Best for active children six yrs. or older; can be too much for little ones

**Other animals:** Better with opposite sex; birds and other small pets fair game

**Abilities:** Obedience, Agility, Terrier races, Earthdog Tests, hunting small game

**Shedding/Grooming:** Minimal if properly groomed; shed in tufts / Pin or slicker brushing, hand stripping, pluck ears for show; use clipper on pets

**Health clearances:** OFA, CERF; **Ask about:** Legg-Perthes, PRA, cataracts, heart defects, epilepsy

**Best with:** Active and experienced owners, fenced yards, hikers, small-game hunters, early socialization and training

***Not for:*** Multiple-dog homes, robotic Obedience, backyard dogs, elderly or sedentary, peaceful, orderly housekeepers

Other than coat, Wires are similar to their Smooth counterparts. Owners describe them as "little tornadoes," musing they must be the inspiration for the term "scatter" rugs. Wires do everything full force, slamming into walls or scrambling over furniture to reach a coveted ball.

They're quick to learn when they want to. For instance, one elderly Wire with failing hearing and eyesight keeps her foot on her owner's while dinner is made so the dog won't miss any treats. Like Smooths, Wires vocalize happiness, loneliness or displeasure.

## Irish Terrier

**Size:** Medium, 18–20", 25–36#

**Color:** Shades of red or wheaten

**Protection:** Strong and intense enough to strike trepidation into intruder's heart

**Energy:** High outdoors, calm inside

**Life expectancy:** 13–16 yrs.

**Children:** Most friendly, love to play

**Other animals:** Tolerate pets, but will not stand for attempts to dominate

**Abilities:** Terrier Trials, upland bird and small-game hunting, Agility

**Shedding/Grooming:** Minimal if groomed properly / Hand stripping twice a year; clipping okay for pets

**Health clearances:** CERF; **Ask about:** Urinary stones, microphthalmia

**Best with:** Action, fences, people strong in mind and body

***Not for:*** Submissive owners, off-leash walks

Playmate, watchdog, footwarmer, hiking companion or daring small game hunter, the Irish is ready and willing. Distinguished when necessary, rowdy if need be, this terrier is capable of almost any role. Check fences frequently for possible escape routes.

An Irish Terrier joke goes, "They're friendly with other animals if the other is submissive or dead." Strange animals are challenged if they stray near the home turf.

## Kerry Blue Terrier

Photo: Downey

**Size:** Medium, F. 17.5–19", 30–35#; M. 18–19.5", 33–40#

**Color:** A distinct blue-gray when mature

**Protection:** Has deep warning bark for trespassers

**Energy:** Medium–high; ready for romp, but peaceful inside

**Life expectancy:** 15–16 yrs.

**Children:** Patient and protective; give slurpy kisses

**Other animals:** Sensible, but typical terrier

**Abilities:** Obedience, Tracking, Terrier Trials, will herd or guard livestock, service fields

**Shedding/Grooming:** Minimal / Brush, comb weekly; trim body and clip head monthly or find someone skilled in the art

**Health clearances:** OFA, CERF; **Ask about:** Cataracts, blood disorders

**Best with:** Early Obedience and socialization, firm direction, long walks or fenced yard

***Not for:*** Sedentary life, the infirm, wishy-washy owners

Versatile according to the owner's desire, Kerries cross into other groups' abilities. These utilitarian dogs guard, herd, hunt, retrieve or go to ground. They're sturdy enough to patrol a ranch and ward off intruders of the two-footed or four-footed variety. Yet they possess the size and sensibility to fit well into condo living.

Kerrys should be taught basic manners early and must learn to recognize their owner as the alpha leader. Once they understand how things work, they'll contentedly go with the flow. The Kerry appears black at birth, graying to a unique blue ideally by eighteen months.

## Lakeland Terrier

**Size:** Medium–small, 13–15", 14–20#

**Color:** Blue, black, liver, red, or wheaten, which may have a saddle of blue, black, liver or grizzle

**Protection:** Moderate, will bark

**Energy:** High

**Life expectancy:** 12–16 yrs.

**Children:** Yes, but may be too active for some

**Other animals:** Aggression level is lower than many terriers; often play well with other animals

**Abilities:** Varmint hunters, Earthdog Tests

**Shedding/Grooming:** Minimal / Hand stripping for show

**Health clearances:** OFA hips and elbows, CERF; **Ask about:** Legg-Perthes, cataracts, lens luxation, vWD

**Best with:** Active owners; sense of humor; firm, consistent, but patient training

***Not for:*** Couch potatoes, pushovers

The Lakeland is active and curious, much like a young child. Their attributes can lead them and their young owners into all sorts of funny or troubling dilemmas. Owners say, "They're con artists and like to get their own way. They'll try to charm you."

Keeping the dog's interest is always a problem with terriers. Like human students, almost anything is more fun than lessons: a bird or a kid on a bike. Lakies are big enough to be sturdy and tough when the situation demands it, but small enough to be portable and easily managed.

## Standard Manchester Terrier

**Size:** Small, F. 12–16#; M. 16–22#

**Color:** Black with mahogany or tan points

**Protection:** Good, keen hearing and sight, wary of strangers

**Energy:** High, but not hysterical

**Life expectancy:** 16–18 yrs.

**Children:** Excellent when raised with them; may be too protective

**Other animals:** Socialize well, prefer their own breed; rarely challenge but won't back down

**Abilities:** Earthdog Tests, Obedience, Tracking, Flyball

**Shedding/Grooming:** Light seasonal shed / Wash-and-wear

**Health clearances:** OFA, CERF; **Ask about:** Legg-Perthes, PRA, VWD, seizures, hypothyroidism

**Best with:** Active owners, persuasive firm training, secure fencing

***Not for:*** Permissive or indulgent owners, extreme cold

Manchesters find home where the heart is. They'll adapt to an apartment, but will use every inch of a 10-acre field when available. If a door opens, they'll take off in search of adventure. Uncensored, they can be barkers.

Almost catlike, they're curious and extremely clean. A Manchester is liable to pop up in strange places. It's not unusual to find one burrowed under the bed covers taking a nap. They're said to like everyone, but love one. That special person has the advantage of a lap and bedwarmer. Standards are more independent than the Toy variety.

## Miniature Bull Terrier

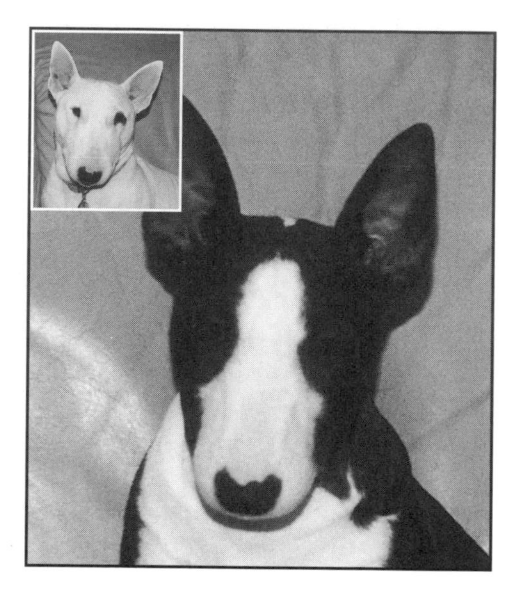

**Size:** Small, 15–35#, F. 12–14"; M. 13–15"

**Color:** White; colored can be any color, including brindle

**Protection:** Low, will bark at really suspicious characters

**Energy:** Moderately active, busy dogs

**Life expectancy:** 10–14 yrs.

**Children:** Happy to play ball forever; may be too rambunctious for little ones

**Other animals:** Most accept, better with less assertive breeds; will harass cats and stalk caged pets

**Abilities:** Obedience, Agility, Flyball, Weight Pulling, Terrier digs, Tracking

**Shedding/Grooming:** Average / Occasional brushing

**Health clearances:** OFA, CERF, BAER (kidney function, heart exam); **Ask about:** Patellar luxation, lens luxation and glaucoma, heart defects, kidney disorder, deafness, laryngeal paralysis

**Best with:** Sense of humor, fences, firm patient owners

***Not for:*** Outdoor life; fastidious or authoritarian owners; soft, timid people; those away from home a lot; too much activity during temperature extremes

The Mini has all the fun, affection and determination of the Bully in a smaller package. Despite their fun-loving outlook on life, Minis are still willful Terriers. Like their bigger siblings, they have sudden bursts of energy—much like a cat—turning the house into a racetrack for a couple laps. With Minis as pets, owners never need go to the circus for entertainment.

Visitors may not be as fond of the enthusiasm of these party animals, so training is advised to curtail unwelcome advances. Minis are not all fun and games, however. They're all business when dispensing with vermin or heaving their well-muscled shoulders into a Weight Pulling harness.

## Miniature Schnauzer

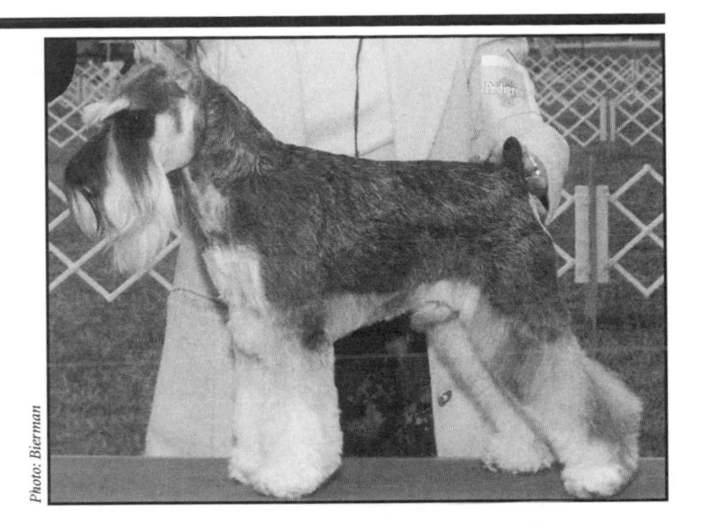

*Photo: Bierman*

**Size:** Small, 12–14", 13–20#

**Color:** Salt and pepper, black and silver, solid black

**Protection:** Will bark

**Energy:** Moderately high

**Life expectancy:** 12–14 yrs.

**Children:** Yes, when raised with them

**Other animals:** Enjoys canine company

**Abilities:** Obedience, Agility

**Shedding/Grooming:** Not much when properly groomed / Weekly brushing, hand stripping or clipping every two months

**Health clearances:** CERF, **Ask about:** Juvenile cataracts, pancreatitis, hypothyroidism, epilepsy, vWD, liver disorders

**Best with:** Regular grooming, attentive owners

***Not for:*** Outside life, overly busy folks, quiet households

The Miniature Schnauzer is not as assertive as the larger ones. Minis can, however, hold their own on alarm tactics, sounding larger than they are. Full of themselves, Schnauzers are busy, inquisitive and eager to be included in activities. Robust and rugged, they enjoy soccer but are sensible enough to curl up beside the chess table.

The breed's compact size means Minis fit in well in small apartments, although their natural urge to bark at every footstep will have to be curtailed. Their credo is "conform and be dull!" Owners are cautioned to clean teeth regularly and schedule veterinary exams, or these little guys may be left gumming their food in middle age.

## Norfolk Terrier

**Size:** Small, 8–10", 11–12#

**Color:** Red, wheaten, black and tan, grizzle

**Protection:** Quick to bark

**Energy:** High

**Life expectancy:** 12–14 yrs.

**Children:** Good with considerate kids; expose in puppyhood

**Other animals:** Usually play well

**Abilities:** Agility, Earthdog Tests, Obedience

**Shedding/Grooming:** Minimal / Hand stripping for show; pets clipped

**Health clearances:** Heart exam; **Ask about:** Collapsing trachea, cardiomyopathy, anesthesia sensitivity

**Best with:** Fenced yard or run, training

***Not for:*** Rough handling, timid souls

Norfolks are curious about anything that moves. They're playful and delight in playing catch or hiking through the woods and burrowing after critters. All feisty terrier, Norfolks are not staid, submissive lap dogs. These little Terriers think like the bigger members of the group. Rain or shine, they're game to walk, run, play, hunt or investigate. They're well suited to an owner who's just as ready to tackle anything anytime, and they don't need three acres to do it.

## Norwich Terrier

Photo: Bierman

**Size:** Small, 10", 10–15#

**Color:** Red, wheaten, black and tan, grizzle

**Protection:** Will bark

**Energy:** Varies as to owner's desires; eager, but not hyper

**Life expectancy:** 12–14 yrs.

**Children:** Yes, when raised with kids

**Other animals:** Enjoy company of other dogs; many live amiably with cats

**Abilities:** Agility, Tracking, Obedience

**Shedding/Grooming:** Minimal / Brush, hand strip for show; pets usually clipped twice a year

**Health clearances:** OFA, heart exam; **Ask about:** Patellar luxation, cardiomyopathy, epilepsy

**Best with:** Patient owners

***Not for:*** Harsh handling, hot and humid weather, outdoor living

Norwich Terriers have the attributes of larger terriers, being gay and fearless. Yet they are rarely yappy and don't require extensive exercise.

The happy little Norwiches don't recognize their size. This spunky terrier has the pride and carriage of much larger dogs.

Although Norwiches are sensitive, apt pupils, wanting to please their owners, sometimes they just can't help themselves. They're Terriers, after all, and always know best! Off-leash, they *can't* be depended on.

## Scottish Terrier

Photos: Mikron

**Size:** Small, 10", F. 18–21#; M. 19–22#

**Color:** Steel or iron gray, brindled or grizzled, black, wheaten or sandy

**Protection:** Territorial

**Energy:** High

**Life expectancy:** 12–14 yrs.

**Children:** Very good with school-age kids; might chase when they run and scream

**Other animals:** Socialize early; may be quarrelsome with same sex

**Abilities:** Earthdog Tests

**Shedding/Grooming:** Minimal / Brushing several times a week; hand stripping for show; pets may be clipped every 3–4 months

**Health clearances:** vWD; **Ask about:** Hypothyroidism, lymphoma

**Best with:** Fenced yard, those in tune to Terrier psyche, training

***Not for:*** Outdoor living, the yard-proud, inattentive or impatient owners

Scotties have experienced the rise and fall of popularity. Now free of the scourge of backyard breeders, the wee Scots are back to the sensible, good-tempered dogs they were bred to be. They can be stubborn and pushy, however, to achieve goals, whether a toy, another treat or an ill-timed jaunt to the park. The Scottie is happiest when his busy-ness is satisfied. A second dog can help siphon the energy.

Training and housebreaking can be a challenge. This obstinate, independent character must be convinced it's your way or no way. On-leash walks or fences are a necessity, but even fences can't confine a determined canine bulldozer or Houdini. Supervision and frequent fence checks solve those problems. Buyers who fall in love with the cute puppy but are unprepared for a determined, self-willed adult are usually the cause of rescue situations.

## Sealyham Terrier

**Size:** Small, 10.5", F, 21–22#; M 23–24#

**Color:** White, with lemon, tan or badger markings

**Protection:** Low, but has a bark much bigger than itself

**Energy:** Medium–low

**Life expectancy:** 12–14 yrs.

**Children:** With older ones; no patience if teased

**Other animals:** Tolerant if raised with them

**Abilities:** Earthdog Tests

**Shedding/Grooming:** Minimal, if properly groomed / A lot—hand stripping for show, clipping for pets

**Health clearances:** CERF, BAER, heart exam; **Ask about:** PRA, cataracts, glaucoma, lens luxation, deafness, spinal problems, heart defect

**Best with:** Patient owners, consistent

***Not for:*** Those too busy or too soft-hearted to discipline

Despite short legs, this breed can move quickly when their mind is set, as when reclaiming the yard from invading rabbits or squirrels. They're perfectly willing to excavate to reach a gopher or mole. Sealys are described as dominant and bull-headed. Reserved with strangers, Sealys are devoted to family and consider themselves on an equal footing. Independent thinkers and self-assured, Sealys are smart, classy companions, not always underfoot. But they're happy to clown and will do almost anything for a cookie.

## Skye Terrier

Photo: Tatham

**Size:** Low height but substantial, 25–40#, F. 10–12"; M. 11–14"

**Color:** Black, blue, gray, silver, fawn, cream

**Protection:** Moderate

**Energy:** Moderate, laid back compared to many Terriers

**Life expectancy:** 12–14 yrs.

**Children:** Older well-behaved children

**Other animals:** Not fond of them; can learn not to eat family cats

**Abilities:** Tracking, Agility, Obedience, Terrier Trials

**Shedding/Grooming:** Yes / Frequent brushing and combing

**Health clearances:** OFA elbows; **Ask about:** Premature closure of radius and ulna, hypothyroidism, perianal fistulas

**Best with:** Fenced yard, early socialization and training, understanding pack order

***Not for:*** Kennel dogs, perfection Obedience, wimps, frail or first-time owners

The shiny, flowing Skye coat belies power hidden beneath, the ability to tackle underground critters that fight viciously for their lives. Instinctively, Skyes can follow their nose into trouble. Hamster types must be kept out of reach. A determined Skye can open the sturdiest cage and perhaps break teeth doing it. Their motto seems to be "Lead, follow, or get out of the way!" Once pack position is established, they usually acquiesce. To minimize stress on growth plates, Skyes should not be allowed to tackle stairs or jump onto hard surfaces until mature (ten months or more).

## Soft Coated Wheaten Terrier

Photo: Cook

**Size:** Medium, F. 17–18", 30–35#; M. 18–19", 35–40#

**Color:** Wheaten

**Protection:** Medium, will bark

**Energy:** Medium–high; mellow with age

**Life expectancy:** 12–14 yrs.

**Children:** Yes, with considerate ones

**Other animals:** Usually accept household pets

**Abilities:** Obedience, Tracking, Agility

**Shedding/Grooming:** Minimal / High maintenance: comb frequently, trim to neaten

**Health clearances:** OFA, CERF, renal function tests; **Ask about:** PRA, cataracts, renal cortical hypoplasia, vWD

**Best with:** High fences, training, consistent and firm discipline

***Not for:*** Outdoor life, submissive owners, easy care

This breed is often passed over in favor of one with a lower-maintenance coat. Just a trek around the yard can attract mud, leaves, snow or burrs. The hair is soft, unlike many harsh-coated Terriers. Wheaties appeal to both men and women, and are described as being pretty, but spunky.

Rarely used by hunters, Wheatens retain terrier instincts. High-spirited, fun dogs, they're friendly enough to follow any person or critter if not fenced. They enjoy being up close and friendly, tending to jump on and greet visitors face-to-face. This jumping ability can be a problem if the combination is a low fence and an inquisitive dog with a chase instinct. Cuddly in appearance, Wheatens are no soft pushovers. Owners must be able to cope with their exuberant temperament and strength of character.

## Staffordshire Bull Terrier

**Size:** Medium, 14–16", F. 24–34#; M. 28–38#

**Color:** Red, fawn, white, black, blue, brindle, may have white markings

**Protection:** Low, but alert

**Energy:** Medium–high

**Life expectancy:** 12–14 yrs.

**Children:** Exceptional, but strong and lively; may jump on little ones

**Other animals:** Play with family pets; supervision suggested

**Abilities:** Obedience, Tracking, Agility, therapy

**Shedding/Grooming:** Some, particularly seasonal / Curry comb

**Health clearances:** OFA, CERF; **Ask about:** Cataracts, entropion

**Best with:** Early training; a social life; strong-minded, fair owners

***Not for:*** The sedentary, outdoor living, running loose, flimsy toys, new dog owners, extreme temperatures

The Staffordshire does everything full throttle: play, work and love. They are willing to join in almost any activity if it's a "proper English day," i.e., not too hot, but no freezing rain. Many people would be unlikely to intrude without invitation, associating the outgoing Staffie with Pit Bulls. This also means the breed has felt the heat and fallout from breed-specific legislation and home insurance discrimination.

Staffies love a challenge and believe variety is the jalapeño of life. Owners need to protect these dogs from injuring themselves. Totally fearless and curious, they're liable to jump off a deck or walk through broken glass. Their powerful jaws tear through a vinyl toy to kill (and sometimes swallow) the squeakie in no time. Tough rubber, rope or nylon toys are the only safe ones.

## Welsh Terrier

**Size:** Medium, 15–15.5", 20–25#

**Color:** Black and tan

**Protection:** Defensive, warning barks and barks and ...

**Energy:** Medium–high

**Life expectancy:** 12–14 yrs.

**Children:** Good with considerate ones; can be impatient with toddlers

**Other animals:** "Regard all suburban wildlife from garter snakes to opossums as potential prey"; sociable with other dogs, but cats are enemies

**Abilities:** Earthdog Trials, lure coursing, Agility, hunting small game, therapy

**Shedding/Grooming:** Minimal, after puppy shed / Brush with slicker, comb; hand stripping, clipping for pets

**Health clearances:** OFA, CERF; **Ask about:** Patellar luxation, glaucoma, distichiasis, lens luxation, cataracts

**Best with:** Obedience school, early socialization, fenced yard or kennel, regular exercise

***Not for:*** Docile pet, by-rote Obedience, tying to doghouse, the sendentary

Calm and sensible, the Welsh is described as "no frills." Sturdy dogs with limitless stamina for fun and games, they're happy to gnaw on chewbones while people play on the computer. A sense of humor helps the owner of this canine comedian with a tendency to mischief. Most Terriers test their limits within the pack, and Welsh are no different. Like kids, the "teens," i.e., puberty, can be particularly trying. Unlike human kids, however, they bend to authority.

Photo: D. Ashbey

## West Highland White Terrier

**Size:** Small, F. 10", 13–18#; M. 11", 15–20#

**Color:** White

**Protection:** Alert, sound alarm

**Energy:** High

**Life expectancy:** 12–14 yrs.

**Children:** Effervescent, fun-loving and sturdy, but introduce early; can be testy with toddlers

**Other animals:** Happy-go-lucky (except with rodentlike pets) but like to be leader

**Abilities:** Earthdog Tests, terrier digs, Tracking, Agility

**Shedding/Grooming:** Very light when properly groomed / Hand strip, clip and scissor pets

**Health clearances:** OFA, CERF; **Ask about:** CMO, Legg-Perthes, cataracts

**Best with:** Active owners, supervised activity and on-leash walks

***Not for:*** Instant Obedience, submissive or sedate owners, off-leash walks

Self-appointed watchdogs, Westies warn the household about everything from an ominous chipmunk to unusual sounds. "Bouncy, boisterous, filled with the joy of living and a light-hearted impudence," the Westie tends to be busy, busy, busy. They rarely give up, demanding attention when they want it, and they're hard to resist. Owners must steel themselves to be firm when necessary and to curtail unnecessary noise. Although bright and eager, these little scamps can be trying in Obedience. A good-humored owner says, "Some trainers have to keep getting new dogs to train."

Hamsters, rabbits and the like are too great a temptation. One mole can call for an excavation of the entire yard. "Westies are white dogs that want to be black. They love digging and being grubby," owners warn.

# Toys

# 7 More Than a Toy (Toys)

From the hairless Chinese Crested to the profusely-coated Pekingese, Toy breeds were bred and kept as elegant companions. They fulfill that role still.

Some Toys are miniatures of their larger counterparts. Not all are as obvious as the Poodle, but the Pug is closely related to Mastiff breeds, the Pomeranian is a tiny version of Spitz and Nordic types, and the Italian Greyhound bears a close resemblance to other Sighthounds.

Personalities vary widely. From the quiet, loving Cavalier King Charles Spaniel to the spunky Brussels Griffon and the clownish Japanese Chin, a Toy breed pleases nearly everybody. These dogs are usually mild mannered and sweet in temperament. While not fearsome in size, their sharp barks may deter an intruder. Even the smallest home can accommodate a Toy—or two or ten! And they fit perfectly into laps. One of their blessings is their longevity. Toys often live to their mid- or late teens, with a few reaching 20 years or more.

Toys are good companions for the elderly or physically challenged because they're easily carried, affectionate and content to snuggle all day if the owner wishes. It's been proven that petting an animal lowers blood pressure. And a pet gives the owner a reason to rise in the morning—in some cases, a reason to live. Tiny dogs are satisfied with a leisurely stroll. A small garden is as big to a Papillon as a park is to a Scottish Deerhound.

Many nursing homes boast a live-in dog, with diminutive breeds often the favorites. Toys fit beside someone in bed or in a wheelchair. Therapy dogs seem to know instinctively which patient needs them the most. Toy breeds don't demand a lot of exercise, have tiny barks, are inexpensive to feed and require less effort in clean-up. In fact, some people who find it difficult to take their pet outside or who live in high-rise apartments teach these minis to use paper or a litter box! Toys are sometimes difficult to housebreak, but perhaps that's because owners tend to spoil them.

These dogs don't weigh a lot and are easily picked up and cuddled, even by arthritic hands. They're agile enough to jump into laps when invited.

Toy breeds aren't just for the elderly. But families with young children are probably better guided to larger dogs able to withstand the assault of toddler tumbles and squooshy hugs. Toys are enthusiastic companions for older kids, snuggling when needed or keeping secrets forever.

Pet owners are advised to look for larger sizes, which may be too big for the ring, but are often sturdier. Toy breeds are rarely sold as early as larger dogs. It's not unusual for breeders to keep pups until they are three or four months old. Since almost all these dogs are under 10 inches, size is often specified by weight. A few are small enough to fit in your pocket, but they're all big enough to fill your heart.

**General characteristics:** Loving, cuddly, spunky, playful, homebodies, devoted to owners. Some can be timid. Must be house pets. Most have desire to please. Good alarms.

Bark: High-pitched in some breeds. Toys talk to owners and each other with their bark.

## Affenpinscher

**Size:** Small, 8–14", average 7–12#

**Color:** Black, gray, silver, black and tan, red

**Protection:** Very alert

**Energy:** Medium–high, busy

**Life expectancy:** 12–14 yrs.

**Children:** Better with older ones

**Other animals:** Introduce early

**Abilities:** Obedience, Agility, will "go to ground" like Terriers

**Shedding/Grooming:** Little / Weekly brushing, some scissoring and clipping or hand stripping

**Health clearances:** OFA, heart exam; **Ask about:** HD, Legg-Perthes, patellar luxation, kidney problems, heart murmurs, hypothyroidism

**Best with:** Experienced trainers, sense of humor

***Not for:*** Small children, easy housebreaking, outdoor living, those wanting mild-mannered Toy dog

Monkeyish in behavior as well as face, Affenpinschers are curious, playful and a bit bossy, tweaking cats' tails and climbing eagerly (even six-foot fences!). They form their own opinions and can be stubborn. Affens are not pushovers. They tend to be possessive of playthings and do not gladly share them with other dogs. Not afraid of big dogs, one Affen stuck her head inquisitively into a yawning Giant Schnauzer's mouth! This nonplussed the Giant, but didn't faze the Affen.

Terrierlike Affens possess many of the same characteristics and personality quirks. Unlike many Toy breeds, Affens don't accept everyone willy-nilly, preferring their family. They're willing to attack an intruder's ankle or put up a raucous fuss. The saucy Affen is sometimes called the "mustached little devil." Breeders warn, "Puppies seem to believe they can fly and fearlessly launch themselves into space from any height." Care must be taken to keep hair out of eyes or corneal ulcers can develop. Owners should watch for retained puppy teeth.

## Brussels Griffon (Rough and Smooth)

Photo: J. Ashbey

**Size:** Small, 8–12#

**Color:** Red, beige, black and tan, black

**Protection:** Can make a lot of noise

**Energy:** Couch decorations with occasional bursts of pep

**Life expectancy:** 12–15 yrs.

**Children:** Yes, better with older ones

**Other animals:** Sensitive, but sensible

**Abilities:** Obedience

**Shedding/Grooming:** Yes / Brush smooths; brush and hand strip or clip roughs

**Health clearances:** OFA, CERF; **Ask about:** Patellar luxation, PRA

**Best with:** Fenced yard, older children

***Not for:*** Outdoor living, rambunctious youngsters

Griffons are climbers and will often be found perched on the backs of furniture. Baby gates are no hindrance. If you want to keep a Griffon out of a room, a closed door or crate will do it, but training is best.

Rough or Smooth, the jaunty Griffon dispenses with vermin as quickly as one of the Terrier group. The large prominent eyes are particularly prone to injury.

## Cavalier King Charles Spaniel

**Size:** Small, 12–13", 12–18#

**Color:** Red and white, tricolor, black and tan, mahogany red

**Protection:** A real people dog, but will bark

**Energy:** Medium

**Life expectancy:** 12–15 yrs.

**Children:** Playful and affectionate with older kids

**Other animals:** Content to accept others as leaders

**Abilities:** Flyball, Agility, Obedience

**Shedding/Grooming:** Moderate / Weekly brushing, combing

**Health clearances:** OFA, CERF, heart exam; **Ask about:** Patellar luxation, cataracts, retinal problems, MVD

**Best with:** Cuddlers, regular grooming, good humor

***Not for:*** Rough play, outside life, robotic Obedience

This little spaniel is spunky enough to play Flyball or go for a hike, but docile enough to sleep on a lap. These dogs retain many of the spaniel hunting instincts and find wildlife fascinating, pointing birds or squirrels. Unlike many Toy dogs, they housebreak easily.

Indiscriminate at showing affection to all family members, Cavs will run around the backyard with a youngster and suffer a doll carriage ride with another. They'll shadow Mom while she's making dinner and watch a football game with Dad.

## Chihuahua (Long Coat and Smooth Coat)

**Size:** Tiny, under 6#

**Color:** Any color

**Protection:** Will bark, willing to back it up but not likely to thwart a bully

**Energy:** Medium–high

**Life expectancy:** 16–18 yrs.

**Children:** With responsible older children

**Other animals:** Enjoy others' company

**Abilities:** Obedience

**Shedding/Grooming:** Long Coats shed seasonally, Smooths all the time / Brush, some scissoring on Long Coat

**Health clearances:** OFA, CERF; **Ask about:** Patellar luxation, PRA, glaucoma, lens luxation, entropion, heart defects, hypoglycemia, tracheal collapse

**Best with:** Daily interaction, gentle handling

***Not for:*** Outdoor life, toddlers

Chihuahuas are often saucy and are described as Terrierlike. They're active and playful, scrambling on furniture, bouncing on cushions. Bold and inquisitive, these tiniest of the tiny can find themselves in trouble if left on their own.

Easily lifted, housed and groomed, Chihuahuas fit conveniently into small quarters. Owners often have more than one. They're often cherished by the elderly, and are sometimes carried in a pocket or purse. These little dogs can be paper or litterbox trained. They do like to chatter among themselves, seeming yappy to some people. Extremely long-lived, Chihuahuas sometimes reach their twenties.

## Chinese Crested (Hairless and Powderpuff)

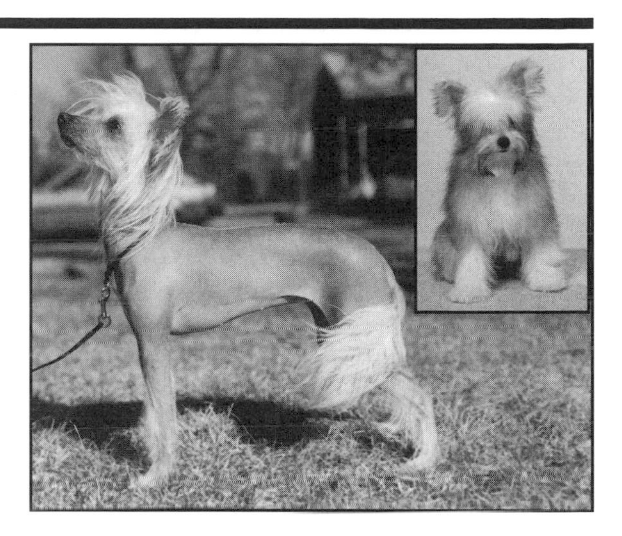

**Size:** Small, 11–13"

**Color:** Any color

**Protection:** Not much

**Energy:** Medium–high

**Life expectancy:** 15–16 yrs

**Children:** Kind, gentle ones

**Other animals:** Loving and playful

**Abilities:** Obedience

**Shedding/Grooming:** Hairless none; Powderpuff minimal / Skin care for Hairless; brushing

**Health clearances:** OFA, CERF; **Ask about:** Legg-Perthes, detached retina, lens luxation

**Best with:** Commitment to skin care, socialization

***Not for:*** Rough handling, ignoring, kennel dogs

The Hairless has tufts of hair only on its head, tip of tail and feet; the Powderpuff has hair on the entire body. Hairless dogs are truly non-shedding and would be a good choice for allergic dog lovers; however, dogs must be wiped with a wet cloth daily, followed by an application of hand lotion. Prone to skin eruptions like human teens, the breed should be bathed at least weekly to avoid blackheads and pimples. A unique feature of the Hairless breeds is their ability to sweat rather than pant when overheated. Dry eyes can be controlled with eye drops.

Bred to dote on their owners, Cresteds shadow family members and prefer to go everywhere with them. Powderpuffs have full dentition while the Hairless variety often has missing teeth, especially premolars. Conscientious dental care is advised to prevent loss of the remaining teeth.

Photo: Shafer

## English Toy Spaniel (Blenheim, Prince Charles/ King Charles, Ruby)

**Size:** Small, F. 8–10#; M. 12–15#

**Color:** Blenheim—red and white; Prince Charles—tricolor/King Charles—black and tan; Ruby—mahogany red

**Protection:** None

**Energy:** Low

**Life expectancy:** 10–12 yrs.

**Children:** Yes, older ones recommend

**Other animals:** Extremely social, enjoy others

**Abilities:** Lapwarming

**Shedding/Grooming:** Minimal / Brush; trim whiskers and hair on feet

**Health clearances:** OFA, CERF; **Ask about:** Patellar luxation, cataracts, inguinal hernias, heart murmurs, anesthesia sensitivity

**Best with:** Loving, calm homes

***Not for:*** Outdoor living, rough handling, small children

The Blenheim and Prince Charles varieties are more active than either the King Charles or Ruby, which tend to be laid back though playful. Called Charlies, these Toys enjoy a romp in the yard, chasing balls and "retrieving" dead birds. Once actually used in hunting, English Toy Spaniels still show hunting instincts but their biggest quarry today is probably mice. The little spaniel is not wimpy, but will pout if slighted. One owner of both Cockers and English Toys says her "Charlies run circles around the Cockers." Submissive to owners and other canines, the English Toy Spaniel lives only to love and be loved in return. They often lie upside down in a person's lap or arms and sleep. Fanciers joke, "This position is the breed's favorite performance event."

## Italian Greyhound

**Size:** Small, 13–15", 8–12#

**Color:** Any color except brindle or tan markings

**Protection:** Will bark at strangers or odd noises

**Energy:** High, mellow as age

**Life expectancy:** 13–15 yrs.

**Children:** Good rapport with gentle kids

**Other animals:** Usually submissive, but can fight for bantamweight title with small canines

**Abilities:** Agility, Obedience

**Shedding/Grooming:** Minimal / Low

**Health clearances:** OFA, CERF;
**Ask about:** Patellar luxation, PRA, autoimmune diseases, seizures

**Best with:** Early socialization, daily attention, fenced yards, gentle owners in tune to Sighthound psyche

***Not for:*** Outdoor or kennel life, unruly children, instant and unerring Obedience

*Photo: D. Magas*

This Sighthound is described as a better candidate for a liberal arts school than a military academy. IGs have no traffic sense and if allowed to run, they're destined to be hit. This slender, racy breed is sturdy with certain caveats. Rough play can injure them. Athletic, their ability to climb and jump can invite trouble. IGs have broken legs by leaping out of windows or off raised surfaces to follow their people or a too-tempting cat.

IGs have a "real dog" bark rather than a yip. Sweaters or jackets are necessary for low-temperature outings. Cordial, but not demonstrative to strangers, IGs are not timid about showing affection to their own people.

## Japanese Chin

**Size:** Tiny, 8–11"

**Color:** Black and white, red and white

**Protection:** Will bark and then invite burglar in

**Energy:** Adaptable

**Life expectancy:** 12–14 yrs.

**Children:** Older, gentle children

**Other animals:** Live in harmony with others

**Abilities:** Therapy

**Shedding/Grooming:** Oh, yes! Seasonal and constant / Combing twice a week; otherwise wash and wear

**Health clearances:** OFA, CERF; **Ask about:** Patellar luxation, PRA, cataracts, gangliosidosis, anesthesia sensitivity, seizures, breathing problems

**Best with:** Close human companionship

***Not for:*** Outdoor life, immaculate housekeepers, hot or humid weather

Active one moment, snoozing the next, Chins like to grab catnaps and, in fact, are compared to felines by owners. They're not as barky as many Toys. Seizures can occur from stress or low blood sugar.

Great company for the lonely, invalids or seniors, Chins are "in your face" dogs and will even follow owners into the shower. Breeders warn this is not a dog for those who do not want animals on furniture. It's said they'll climb bookcases or seemingly insurmountable objects like a fireplace, to lie decoratively on the mantel. Funny and happy, they originally entertained Oriental aristocracy, much like miniature Kabuki dancers. Bouncy and playful, yet quiet when necessary, they're good apartment dogs.

## Maltese

Photo: D. Ashbey

**Size:** Tiny, 4–6#

**Color:** White

**Protection:** Will bark (in excitement!)

**Energy:** High

**Life expectancy:** 12–15 yrs

**Children:** Above the age of six

**Other animals:** Can be bossy; not good with large animals

**Abilities:** Obedience, Tracking

**Shedding/Grooming:** Minimal / Daily brushing; show coats "wrapped" and tied up at home; pets often trimmed

**Health clearances:** OFA, CERF, BAER; **Ask about:** Patellar luxation, PRA, entropion, glaucoma, hypothyroidism, hypoglycemia, deafness

**Best with:** Fenced yard; affectionate, attentive people

***Not for:*** Outdoor living, small children, roughhousing

The immaculate coat of a show Maltese is a picture. But this doesn't come without dedication and *maximum* care. These white beauties look like angels, and can charm owners into spoiling them. But the devil can turn them into imps. The feisty Maltese is liable to tackle a much larger dog.

Little dogs have the same number of teeth as giants, and 42 teeth crowded into a tiny mouth equals dental problems. Frequent dental care, including brushing by owners and cleaning by veterinarians, is advisable.

## Toy Manchester Terrier

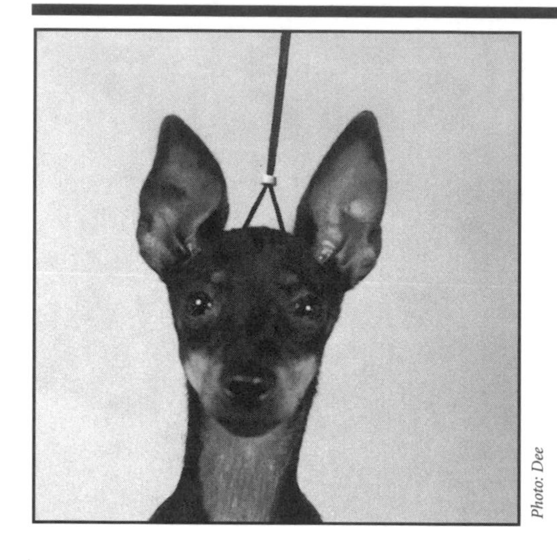
Photo: Dee

**Size:** Tiny, under 12#

**Color:** Black with mahogany, tan

**Protection:** Good, keen hearing and sight; wary of strangers

**Energy:** High

**Life expectancy:** 14–20 yrs.

**Children:** Older children better; may be protective

**Other animals:** Prefer own breed, rarely challenge others

**Abilities:** Earthdog Tests, Obedience, Tracking, Flyball

**Shedding/Grooming:** Light / Brushing

**Health clearances:** OFA, CERF; **Ask about:** Legg-Perthes, PRA, vWD, hypothyroidism, seizures

**Best with:** Active owners; persuasive, firm training; secure fencing

***Not for:*** Small children, heavy-handed methods, permissive or indulgent owners, extreme cold

A scaled-down version of the Standard Manchester, the Toy Manchester has similar attributes. They'll adapt to an apartment, but will use every inch of a 10-acre field if available. If a door opens, they'll take off in search of adventure. A determined ratter, this slim Terrier excels at going to ground. Creepy-crawly things are endangered species, and even birds aren't safe on the ground. Strangers are tolerated at arm's length, particularly when the dog is cozied up to the owner.

Almost catlike, they're curious and extremely clean. They're said to like everyone but love one, tending to bond more closely to one member of the family. That special person has the advantage of a lap- and bedwarmer.

## Miniature Pinscher

**Size:** Tiny, 10–12.5"

**Color:** Black or chocolate with red markings, solid red

**Protection:** Will raise a ruckus

**Energy:** High

**Life expectancy:** 14–15 yrs.

**Children:** If raised with them and children are gentle

**Other animals:** Will hold their own, feisty

**Abilities:** Obedience, Agility

**Shedding/Grooming:** Minimal / Brush and a promise

**Health clearances:** OFA, CERF; **Ask about:** Patellar luxation, Legg-Perthes, PRA, cataracts, pannus

**Best with:** Fencing, active households, secure confinement

***Not for:*** Beginners, rough handling, outdoor living

Toddlerlike, the Min Pin is always busy and into things that could be harmful. Secure the dog in an ex-pen, crate or fenced yard when the door is left open, such as when carrying in groceries. This little dog can squeeze through a minute opening in a flash and be across a road or in it. Many owners have "Min Pin" gates or screens installed in doorways. Fences should be checked for security. Put small ingestible items into drawers, or a midnight run to the vet could be necessary. Squeak toys are too much like mice, liable to be torn apart and swallowed. The Miniature Pinscher is lively and fearless. Its curiosity and energy are reminiscent of terriers.

Although clowning in the ring is a temptation, Min Pins can be sterling performers when tuned in and turned on. The breed's distinguishing hackney gait draws attention as it prances around a ring or down the street.

## Papillon

**Size:** Tiny, 10–12", 5–9#

**Color:** Particolor (mostly white)

**Protection:** Will bark . . . and bark

**Energy:** High

**Life expectancy:** 14–15 yrs.

**Children:** Older, gentle children

**Other animals:** Enjoys others, but takes alpha role

**Abilities:** Obedience par excellence, Agility, Flyball

**Shedding/Grooming:** Little / Comb or brush frequently

**Health clearances:** OFA, CERF; **Ask about:** Patellar luxation, PRA or other eye problems

**Best with:** Active, fun-loving owners; positive training

***Not for:*** Outdoor life, TV addicts, small or rowdy children

With big hearts in small bodies, Paps are willing to take on tasks too big for them. Their attitude is "Sure, I'll climb the mountain with you!" Attention span is exceptional; Paps like to listen to their owners. When grown, they'll watch you for extended periods as long as you talk to them. They enjoy working or playing with their owners and are easily trainable.

Like other tiny dogs, the Papillon has a tiny mouth with a full count of 42 teeth. Discuss a dental care plan with the dog's breeder and veterinarian.

## Pekingese

**Size:** Small, under 6–14#

**Color:** Red, fawn, black, black and tan, sable, brindle, white, particolor

**Protection:** Will bark up a storm

**Energy:** Low

**Life expectancy:** 13–15 yrs.

**Children:** Older, quieter children

**Other animals:** Strictly individualistic

**Abilities:** Therapy

**Shedding/Grooming:** Seasonal / Weekly with bristle brush and comb

**Health clearances:** OFA, CERF; **Ask about:** Pastern or patellar luxation, eye injuries, dry eye, spinal problems

**Best with:** Gentle handling, patient training

***Not for:*** Outdoor living, active people, heavy exercise, small children, hot and humid weather

The Pekingese has a lionlike, regal dignity, full of self-importance, confidence and "exasperating stubbornness." Pekes seem to have an air of mystery about them, reminiscent of their ancient Oriental history. They can be difficult to train. After all, they're royalty; why should they do something their subjects want? Owners need to win respect without spoiling—easy to do. The tiniest Pekes, barely tipping the scales at five pounds or under, are called "sleeves," for where their Chinese masters carried them.

Normally low-key, Pekes can be lively at times and comical when they want to be. Usually their philosophy is "Let someone else do it, and I'll watch." Perfectly content to supervise from the comfort of a chair, the Peke likes to oversee activity and direct people from his throne. Like other brachycephalic breeds, the Peke tends to snort and snore while taking one of many catnaps.

## Pomeranian

**Size:** Tiny, 3–7#

**Color:** Red, orange, cream and sable, black, brown and blue, particolor

**Protection:** Alert, will bark

**Energy:** High

**Life expectancy:** 12–17 yrs.

**Children:** Yes, with children over six yrs.

**Other animals:** Social, but willing to tackle larger animals—which can be their undoing

**Abilities:** Obedience, therapy

**Shedding/Grooming:** Some / Moderate, brushing

**Health clearances:** OFA, CERF; **Ask about:** Patellar luxation, PRA, cataracts, entropion, hypoglycemia, tracheal collapse, PDA

**Best with:** Gentle handling, fences, frequent dental care

***Not for:*** Outdoor life, small children or rough play

Poms tend to "talk" a lot, voicing their opinion about everything. These little dogs are always busy, announcing visitors, peering into shopping bags, or bustling about checking on the family members' whereabouts. A foxy face can often be seen peering out of a backpack or a handbag. As wee descendants of Nordic dogs, Poms love to run. With such a tiny breed, they can easily squeeze through the smallest opening and be lost or crushed by a car.

## Toy Poodle

Photo: D. Gossett

**Size:** Tiny, up to 10"

**Color:** Blue, gray, silver, brown, cafe-au-lait, apricot, cream

**Protection:** Will bark

**Energy:** High

**Life expectancy:** 12–14 yrs.

**Children:** Older, sensible children

**Other animals:** Social and playful

**Abilities:** Obedience

**Shedding/Grooming:** Almost none, sheds within coat / Extensive, must be clipped regularly

**Health clearances:** OFA, CERF; **Ask about:** Patellar luxation, cataracts, PRA, epilepsy, hypoglycemia

**Best with:** Lots of attention, professional grooming

***Not for:*** Outdoor life, toddlers, aggressive youngsters

Like bigger siblings, the littlest Poodle is active, playful, loving and bonds closely with owners. The breed is tractable and eager to please. Toys are harder to find than Minis and Standards. The so-called "teacup" Poodle is *not* an approved size, but only a commercial label to enhance sales. Dwarfed teacups more commonly have exaggerated health and anatomical problems.

Some people tend to treat Toys as spoiled children, which leads some owners into feeding filet mignon or breast of quail exclusively. But one owner says, "My Poodles fight over grapes and you can't eat a bowl of cereal (and fruit) at our house without contending with sorrowful eyes and wistful sighs." (See Standard and Miniature.)

## Pug

**Size:** Small, 10–11", 14–18#

**Color:** Silver, apricot-fawn, black

**Protection:** Will bark a little

**Energy:** Low

**Life expectancy:** 12–14 yrs.

**Children:** Playful and loving

**Other animals:** Usually placid

**Abilities:** Obedience, therapy

**Shedding/Grooming:** Continually / Rub daily with hound glove; clean facial wrinkles

**Health clearances:** OFA, CERF; **Ask about:** Legg-Perthes, PRA, cataracts, entropion, eye injuries, epilepsy, liver disease, anesthesia sensitivity

**Best with:** Air-conditioning, interaction, homebodies

***Not for:*** Outdoor living, ignoring, harsh commands, hot and humid weather

The sturdy Pug knows no enemies and would be totally useless in warding off a burglar. Pugs like to be close to you, but are unobtrusive. They'll often snuggle at your feet and contentedly snore. They "blimp out" quickly, so owners must watch their pets' diet and encourage exercise. Dry eye is sometimes a problem with the breed. Owners can help alleviate the discomfort with artificial tears.

The Pug has a dignity that would fit into the lifestyle of royalty. Yet they are natural clowns and good for an evening's entertainment.

## Shih Tzu

**Size:** Small, 8–11", 9–16#

**Color:** Any color

**Protection:** Will bark, but basically friendly

**Energy:** Medium–low

**Life expectancy:** 10–14 yrs.

**Children:** Yes

**Other animals:** Lovers, not fighters

**Abilities:** Shadow

**Shedding/Grooming:** Minimal / Regular brushing and combing

**Health clearances:** OFA, CERF, kidney function tests; **Ask about:** Renal cortical hypoplasia, autoimmune hemolytic anemia, vWD

**Best with:** Protection from the heat, grooming care

***Not for:*** Outdoor living, small children, Obedience fanatics

Accepting of new people and situations, the Shih Tzu is not fickle, but loves life along with almost everyone. The beautiful, flowing coat gives a regal bearing. But Shih Tzus are not above doing a comedy routine, endearing themselves to owners even more. These dogs enjoy everything from camping to fetching tennis balls.

Friendly and outgoing, the breed is a hit as a therapy dog. The sweet Shih Tzu can cuddle in a lap, listen to whispered memories or do tricks.

## Silky Terrier

**Size:** Tiny–small, 9–10", 10#

**Color:** Blue and tan

**Protection:** Alert, will bark

**Energy:** High

**Life expectancy:** 15–16 yrs.

**Children:** Yes, introduce early

**Other animals:** Some are testy with other dogs

**Abilities:** Loving

**Shedding/Grooming:** Minimal / Damp brushing every few days

**Health clearances:** OFA; **Ask about:** Patellar luxation, diabetes, epilepsy, tracheal collapse

**Best with:** Exercise, socialization, frequent grooming

***Not for:*** Outdoor living; a silent, sedentary pet

The Silky is a terrier, albeit a tiny one, and can dig or scamper after an enticing critter if left to its own resources. The soprano bark greets every visitor, so apartment residents need to teach them to be selective about ringing those chimes. Some like to schmooze with everyone, people or other animals. Like children, they're cute and easy to spoil so need to be taught boundaries through Obedience and manners.

## Yorkshire Terrier

Photo: J. Ludwig

**Size:** Tiny, 3–7#

**Color:** Blue and rich golden tan

**Protection:** Shrill alarms

**Energy:** High

**Life expectancy:** 12–14 yrs.

**Children:** Okay with older children; can't take rough play

**Other animals:** Like to run show, will challenge even Rottweilers or Great Danes

**Abilities:** Obedience

**Shedding/Grooming:** Very little / Extensive brushing

**Health clearances:** OFA; **Ask about:** Patellar luxation, hypoglycemia, liver shunts

**Best with:** Active but gentle families

***Not for:*** Small children, outdoor life

Born black and tan, the black silvers to blue as the puppy matures. Merry and spunky, the littlest terrier is a good companion for those who enjoy an inquisitive, busy buddy. They're easily portable. In fact, one owner takes her three Yorkies in a backpack when she goes biking.

Owners must remember these are Terriers and need firm, fair discipline. Described as perpetual two-year-olds, Yorkies can be manipulative and will take advantage of their high rating on the adorable scale.

# Non-Sporting Dogs

# 8

# Potpourri (Non-Sporting Dogs)

Dogs were once neatly classified as Sporting, so when these breeds came upon the scene, they were dubbed Non-Sporting—a lackluster name for delightful dogs! Tracing each back to various roots would enable us to classify them easily into another group. But old habits die hard, and they remain Non-Sporting. With gun dogs, retrievers, Mastiffs, spaniels, Nordic dogs and more forming ancestral backgrounds, their sizes, personalities and profiles are wonderfully diversified.

Because they were developed for so many reasons, dogs in this group have varying instincts and don't share characteristics. Other than the Standard and Miniature Poodle varieties, each is a distinct individual.

Ears, tails and coats are as varied as the canines they're attached to. Each breed has a distinctive bark and reasons for doing so, from the relatively quiet French Bulldog to the exuberant Finnish Spitz. From the peppy Dalmatian to the bouncy Lhasa Apso and docile, patient Bulldog, there's a Non-Sporting dog to fit almost every taste.

**General characteristics:** A dog to suit every taste.

Bark: a wide range from soprano to bass.

*Photo: Garden Studio*

## American Eskimo Dog

**Size:** Tiny–medium; Toy 9–12", Miniature 12–15", Standard >15"

**Color:** White, white with biscuit cream

**Protection:** Will raise the roof, puts up ferocious act

**Energy:** High, especially smaller sizes; mellows with age

**Life expectancy:** 13–15 yrs.

**Children:** Okay, with mutual respect; not patient with poking and prodding by toddlers

**Other animals:** Usually accept, but spats sometimes occur

**Abilities:** Obedience, Agility, therapy, Tracking

**Shedding/Grooming:** Heavy / Routine brushing

**Health clearances:** OFA, CERF; **Ask about:** Patellar luxation, PRA, epilepsy, diabetes

**Best with:** Fenced yard; calm, structured environment; patient, active owners; lots of chewies

***Not for:*** Fussy owners, workaholics, pristine landscapes, small or unruly children

Hot summer days will probably find this breed inside next to the air-conditioning duct or digging a hole in the yard to find a cool place. Some owners mention that Eskies are particularly difficult to housebreak until their attention span and bladder control increase. The Eskie is independent and sassy and tends not to be afraid of anything.

American Eskimo Dogs prefer adults to kids. Eskies want to be the center of attention and can become jealous of love and bonding between parents and kids, particularly babies. Because the breed tends to be highly active, excitable children intensify the activity level. The Eskie learns lessons easily and performs tricks to entertain the family. It's said they're also good at reversing the training, and most owners are not even aware they are being trained. The famous "smile" charms owners.

## Bichon Frise

Photo: Booth by Ritter

**Size:** Small, 9.5–11.5", 14–16#

**Color:** White

**Protection:** Announce visitors

**Energy:** Moderate

**Life expectancy:** 14 yrs.

**Children:** Yes, playful and happy

**Other animals:** Content with others ruling

**Abilities:** Obedience, Agility

**Shedding/Grooming:** Minimal / Extensive daily brushing, occasional trimming

**Health clearances:** OFA, CERF; **Ask about:** Patellar luxation, PRA, cataracts, epilepsy, bleeding disorders

**Best with:** Indoor living, frequent grooming

***Not for:*** Outdoorsy, macho owners; isolation

Happy-go-lucky Bichons are accepting of everyone: visitors, children, seniors, invalids and dogs from Great Danes to Maltese. If confronted, they'll roll over as if to say "Do what you will," then crouch with the universal gesture of friendship—a tail wag. Breeders warn they can be hard to housetrain, and this chore takes patience.

Undemanding companions, Bichons are moderate in almost every way except coat care. Active when you want a playmate, they're quiet when you're busy. They'll cuddle when invited, entertain guests or take a nap while you read. Their sparkling eyes and personalities win many friends.

## Boston Terrier

**Size:** Small, <15–25#

**Color:** Brindle, seal or black, all with white markings

**Protection:** Too small for bodyguard; warns with bark but not yappy

**Energy:** Moderately high, mellows with age

**Life expectancy:** 10–14 yrs.

**Children:** Excellent

**Other animals:** Usually accepting

**Abilities:** Agility, Obedience

**Shedding/Grooming:** Minimal / Low maintenance

**Health clearances:** OFA, CERF, BAER;
**Ask about:** Patellar luxation, cataracts, epilepsy, heart anomalies, deafness, eye injuries

**Best with:** Fenced yard, positive reinforcement, loads of attention and lap time

***Not for:*** Outdoor kenneling, temperature extremes, rough children

This American original is outgoing and friendly. The Boston trusts everyone and is liable to leave the yard to follow a child or an inviting adult. These dogs make loving companions for the elderly or invalids. Short-faced breeds should be watched for breathing difficulties if play becomes too exuberant or prolonged.

Always dressed in a formal tux, Bostons are known as the American gentlemen and learn manners quickly. The Boston appreciates a coat or sweater in winter and will often be found snuggling under the covers. Snoring goes along with the shortened muzzle.

## Bulldog

Photo: Booth

**Size:** Medium–large, 40–60#

**Color:** Red brindle, brindle, white, red, fawn, fallow, piebald

**Protection:** Low, but prizefighter mug can scare off an intruder

**Energy:** Low

**Life expectancy:** 8–9 yrs.

**Children:** Excellent; loving but not active

**Other animals:** Usually harmonious; some same-sex aggression

**Abilities:** Loving companionship, walking to the food bowl

**Shedding/Grooming:** Yes / Brush, frequently clean skin folds above nose and around screw tail

**Health clearances:** OFA, CERF, heart exam; **Ask about:** Cataracts, ectropion, entropion, dry eye, elongated palate, heart defects, hypothyroidism

**Best with:** Relaxed households, air-conditioning

***Not for:*** Active or fastidious owners, extreme temperatures, loners

Sleeping is this breed's favorite activity. Eating is next, but they do love a good belly rub. They'll be comforting when you're down and can be clowns. Nobody can wiggle like a happy Bully. They absolutely, positively can't be forced to do something. It's best to make them believe it's their idea. Their tenacity is legion. Bulldogs were bred to hang on in the face of death.

After drinking, they carry water in their jowls, slobbering across the floor. A sense of humor about the breed's propensity for flatulence is a good idea. A large majority of Bulldogs are dysplastic. Selecting pets from lines with athletic builds may help avoid clinical symptoms. C-section deliveries and high puppy mortality make these dogs hard to find and expensive to buy.

## Chinese Shar Pei

**Size:** Medium, 18–20", 40–65#

**Color:** Solid colors

**Protection:** High, raise a racket; can be overprotective

**Energy:** Moderate, rises or sinks with owner's wishes

**Life expectancy:** 7–12 yrs.

**Children:** Strictly an individual trait; socialize early

**Other animals:** Introduce early, some fight contenders and look for challenges; interspecies aggression

**Abilities:** Obedience, Tracking, Agility, therapy

**Shedding/Grooming:** Yes / Brush; clean ears frequently

**Health clearances:** OFA, CERF; **Ask about:** Entropion, demodectic mange, amyloidosis, hypothyroidism, bloat, malabsorption, autoimmune diseases

**Best with:** Socialization, confident owners strong in mind and body

***Not for:*** Overly permissive or submissive people, latchkey dogs

Someone with a Shar Pei is never lonely or at a loss for conversation. With the breed's wrinkles and blue-black tongue, they always attract attention. Owners must establish dominance from the time they bring their puppy home. The breed can be headstrong.

Breeders suggest feeding a low protein diet (less than 17 percent) to forestall kidney problems. Conscientious fanciers fund studies to combat amyloidosis, the cause of the wide range of lifespan. Buyers should choose lines with a known history of healthy animals and that boast longevity. Some Shar Pei pups require "tacking" of the wrinkles around the eyes until they grow into their skin. If this surgery is necessary, the animal cannot be shown. Knowledgeable breeders will inform buyers whether this is necessary.

## Chow Chow (Rough and Smooth)

Photo: Pets by Paulette

**Size:** Medium, 17–20", F. 50–65#; M 60–75#

**Color:** Red, black, blue, cinnamon, cream

**Protection:** High; domain-protective, natural guard

**Energy:** Low

**Life expectancy:** 8–12 yrs.

**Children:** Tolerate if exposed early, but not playful

**Other animals:** Dominant, two males likely to have preliminary bouts or out-and-out brawls

**Abilities:** Agility, Obedience

**Shedding/Grooming:** Seasonal / Rough—daily brushing a must for health; Smooth—wash and wear; comb A LOT during shedding

**Health clearances:** OFA, CERF; **Ask about:** OCD, patellar luxation, PRA, glaucoma, entropion, stenotic nares, hypothyroidism, renal cortical hypoplasia

**Best with:** Confident people; early socialization; firm, fair discipline

***Not for:*** Active playmates, tying outside, outdoor activity in heat

Reserved and dignified, Chows believe most doggy chores are beneath them. The description "lordly" fits. A distinctive feature of the breed is the blue-black tongue.

Other species may be greeted with a growl or ignored as subservient. Breeders advise looking for a happy, confident, easygoing puppy. Chow Chows are quiet, independent, not clinging or hyper, perfectly willing to take a nap while you're busy.

## Dalmatian

**Size:** Medium–large, 19–24", 45–70#

**Color:** White with black or liver spots

**Protection:** Moderate

**Energy:** High, bred to run for miles

**Life expectancy:** 11–13 yrs.

**Children:** Affectionate and patient when raised with them

**Other animals:** Companionable with most, especially horses; birds and yard critters fair game

**Abilities:** Road Trials, flushing and retrieving, Obedience, Tracking, Agility

**Shedding/Grooming:** Year-round, hair sticks everywhere / Brush frequently with rubber curry comb

**Health clearances:** OFA, BAER test, uric acid test; **Ask about:** PRA, glaucoma, diabetes, deafness, uvate bladder stones

**Best with:** Active owners, plenty of exercise, fenced yard, training and socialization, a sense of humor

***Not for:*** Impatient or sedentary people, fussbudget housekeepers, allergy sufferers

Dal puppies are wiggly, kissy examples of perpetual motion. Bric-a-brac can quickly become bric-a-broken. Current popularity, due to Disney's *101 Dalmatians,* has landed this breed into the backyard of puppy mill operators and grab-a-buck owners. Buyers are cautioned to carefully choose only knowledgeable breeders, those who breed for improvement and to avoid health and temperament problems.

Breeders suggest feeding Dals a diet low in protein to combat high uric acid and urate stones. With manners and a couple of brisk romps a day, the Dal's natural exuberance is delightful. Without training, the dog can be obnoxious. Dals tend to prefer one person and tail the favored one around the house. Owners look before walking so they don't trip over their canine shadow.

## Finnish Spitz

**Size:** Medium, F. 15.5–18", 23#; M. 17.5–20", 29#

**Color:** Shades of golden red

**Protection:** Will raise the roof with warnings

**Energy:** Adjusts to owner's lifestyle

**Life expectancy:** 13–14 yrs.

**Children:** Excellent, curious and ready for action

**Other animals:** Generally accept household pets, prefer being leader, some same-sex jealousy and spats

**Abilities:** Hunting

**Shedding/Grooming:** Seasonal / Brushing

**Health clearances:** OFA, CERF; **Ask about:** Cataracts

**Best with:** Reward training, interaction, hunters

***Not for:*** Instant response, kennel dogs, a silent breed, military training methods

Although other members of the family are accepted, it's for one special person that the Finkie's eyes sparkle and tail wags faster. The Spitz is a clean dog, washing that foxy red-gold coat like a cat. Independent and self-willed, this dog performs better for a master, whether showing, hunting or any other task.

A happy Finkie "talks" with little barks and throaty purrs. Close neighbors may object if the Finkie household has heavy human or critter traffic, for the dog can bark 160 times a minute! Training when to bark and when not to is part of a proper upbringing.

## French Bulldog

**Size:** Small, 11–14", 20–28#

**Color:** A variety—most common are black brindle, cream, black-masked fawn, pied

**Protection:** Will bark

**Energy:** Moderate

**Life expectancy:** 10 yrs.

**Children:** Sturdy and friendly

**Other animals:** Plays well, males can be dog-aggressive

**Abilities:** Obedience

**Shedding/Grooming:** Little, seasonal / Weekly brushing, wipe wrinkles

**Health clearances:** OFA, CERF, vWD; **Ask about:** Elbow dysplasia, patellar luxation, cataracts, entropion, elongated soft palate, spinal abnormalities, stenotic nares

**Best with:** Indoor living, air-conditioning

***Not for:*** Joggers or hikers, extreme temperatures, isolation

The Frenchies' bat ears and flat face give these dogs a comical look. And they love to clown as well. Frenchies have the heart, humor and friendliness of the Bulldog all in a convenient, economy-sized package.

Quiet and agreeable, they're often a choice for senior citizens as well as young families. Because they're expensive to breed, their purchase price is higher than some more common breeds.

## Keeshond

Photo: J. Ashbey

**Size:** Medium, F. 17", 35#; M. 18", 40–45#

**Color:** Gray tipped with black, cream furnishings

**Protection:** Friendly, but will bark

**Energy:** Medium–high

**Life expectancy:** 12–15 yrs.

**Children:** Excellent, curious and busy

**Other animals:** Accepted with aplomb

**Abilities:** Agility, Obedience, Tracking, Flyball, Scent Hurdles, therapy

**Shedding/Grooming:** Seasonal / At least weekly brushing and combing; daily during shed

**Health clearances:** OFA; **Ask about:** Patellar luxation, CERF, cataracts (non-progressive), hypothyroidism, epilepsy

**Best with:** Sense of humor, regular grooming, close relationship with their "family"

***Not for:*** Outdoor living, fussbudgets, intimidation

Although lively, Kees are not perpetual motion machines. They join in family activities, then may crash on the couch.

Breeders say Keeshonden are friendly with everyone and affectionate almost to the point of annoyance. Sometimes owners have to curtail the nudge-pat, nudge-pat sequence with a firm "Lie down," at which the chastened pet sighs and lies close by their feet. Females may be more independent than males.

## Lhasa Apso

Photo: Fall

**Size:** Small, F. 9–10", 13–15#; M. 10–11", 15–18#

**Color:** All colors

**Protection:** Great alarms, greet visitors with gusto

**Energy:** Low–moderate

**Life expectancy:** 14 yrs.

**Children:** Depends on individual

**Other animals:** Often bossy

**Abilities:** Supervisor

**Shedding/Grooming:** Minimal / Extensive daily brushing, weekly bathing; neglect will turn into one large mat; a cut-down, shorter coat for pets is common

**Health clearances:** OFA, CERF; **Ask about:** Patellar luxation, PRA, cataracts, entropion, vWD, intervertebral disk disease

**Best with:** Early socialization and training, dedicated groomers

***Not for:*** Outdoor living, waggy acceptance of everyone

When a person enters, Lhasas will greet friends with glee, but are aloof with strangers until adequate introductions are made. Like little children, Lhasas show off for company, dropping a toy in a friendly lap. They're said to play the clown, but never the fool. They have a distinct talent for making an unwanted visitor feel lower than dirt. However, when that person is finally accepted, it is as though royal favor has been bestowed.

Some pet owners and fanciers with retired show dogs elect to clip the coats. "When shorn, they lose all their regal dignity, running around like a giddy pup for a few laps of the yard."

## Miniature Poodle

**Size:** Small, 10–15", 12–20#

**Color:** Blue, gray, silver, brown, cafe-au-lait, apricot, cream

**Protection:** Low, but will bark

**Energy:** High

**Life expectancy:** 14–16 yrs.

**Children:** Excellent with older ones

**Other animals:** After establishing pack position, forget royal status and play well

**Abilities:** Obedience, Agility

**Shedding/Grooming:** Nearly none / High maintenance; clip and scissor, often done professionally; pluck ear hair

**Health clearances:** OFA, CERF; **Ask about:** Legg-Perthes, patellar luxation, PRA, cataracts, glaucoma, PDA, deafness, gangliosidosis, epilepsy

**Best with:** Committed groomers, Intense bonding

***Not for:*** Ignoring, kennel life

Photo: D. Gossett

Minis are small enough to obtain their exercise running around an apartment—and, with their grace, they don't make a lot of noise doing it. Yet they're sturdy enough to jog two miles a day. Many love to clamber on top of furniture, perching on the back, probably the better to survey their kingdom.

Extremely adaptable and capable, the Poodle will try almost anything an owner wants. Minis swim well, and thanks to their heritage, will retrieve from water—or at least a ball from a swimming pool. (See also Standard.)

## Standard Poodle

**Size:** Large, F. 22–25", 40–65#; M. 24–27", 50–80#

**Color:** Blue, gray, silver, brown, cafe-au-lait, apricot, cream

**Protection:** Moderate, will bark and stand their ground

**Energy:** Boundless, but calm and relaxed house pets

**Life expectancy:** 10–13 yrs.

**Children:** Excellent, though puppy may be too much for toddler or reserved child

**Other animals:** Play well when pack order established

**Abilities:** Water and upland fowl retrieving, Obedience, Tracking, Agility, performers, service fields

**Shedding/Grooming:** Almost non-existent with proper grooming, good for allergic people / Exhaustive daily grooming with metal comb and slicker and pin brushes, clip and scissor every four to six weeks; many owners elect professional care

**Health clearances:** OFA, CERF, vWD, skin punch for SA; **Ask about:** PRA, cataracts, entropion, epilepsy, bloat, SA, Addison's disease, renal cortical hypoplasia

**Best with:** Fenced yards, wannabe hairdressers, interaction, enough $$$$ for pro grooming, confident owners

***Not for:*** Ignoring, people who are gone a lot

These athletes enjoy frequent outdoor exercise. They don't mind heat and love to play in snow, but ice and snow cling to coats. A team of Standards actually ran the Iditarod! Contrary to the opinion that a sissy exists under the pompadour, Poodles are courageous, not wimpy.

When a Poodle loves, the owner will never be lonely. The breed is highly sensitive and seems to know when you need a look of adoration sent your way. Owners state, "A Poodle that is constantly lethargic is either very ill or NOT a Poodle." (See also Miniature.)

## Schipperke

*Photo: Booth*

**Size:** Small, <18#, F 10–12"; M 11–13"

**Color:** Black

**Protection:** Alert and spunky, with sharp bark; will not back down

**Energy:** High

**Life expectancy:** 12–15 yrs.

**Children:** Happy and playful with friendly ones; introduce early

**Other animals:** Territorial with unfamiliar ones

**Abilities:** Hunting small game, Agility, Obedience

**Shedding/Grooming:** Seasonal, voluminous / Minimal, some brushing, more during shed

**Health clearances:** OFA, CERF; **Ask about:** Legg-Perthes, PRA, cataracts, entropion, hypothyroidism, epilepsy

**Best with:** Active owners, training, fences, protection from heat

***Not for:*** Isolation, a dull life, off-leash walks, quiet and docile lap dog

The Schip can be a scamp, always alert and full of fun, not above a bit of mischief. Life is an adventure! Schips are inquisitive and fearless of heights, cars and strange places, so owners must be cautious and protect these impish dogs from their own derring-do and devil-made-me-do-it outlook on life.

Schips are cooperative if taught their place in the family. Some owners say their independence can make them difficult to housebreak and leads them to tussle over nail trimming.

## Shiba Inu

**Size:** Small–medium, 18–25#, F. 13.5–15.5"; M. 14.5–16.5"

**Color:** Red, red sesame, black and tan, black sesame, brindle; may have white markings

**Protection:** Territorial, will bark

**Energy:** Moderate and adjustable

**Life expectancy:** 12–15 yrs.

**Children:** Yes, when raised with them

**Other animals:** Sex-specific aggression; invaders will be challenged

**Abilities:** Small game hunting, Tracking

**Shedding/Grooming:** Seasonal / Minimal, some brushing; more during shed

**Health clearances:** OFA; **Ask about:** Patellar luxation, hypothyroidism

**Best with:** Fenced yards, constant people contact, early and continuous training and socialization

***Not for:*** Isolation, off-leash runs, milquetoast owners, instant or top-scoring Obedience

Shibas are bold, spirited, alert and good-natured—but very much a dominant breed. Shiba puppies are often alpha and must have consistent discipline. Not a cuddly dog, the Shiba is catlike and aloof with strangers. They keep themselves clean and require little grooming except during the intense shed.

Shibas determine whether or not to obey. The cute little fluffball puppy grows into a strong, independent dog. Almost anything is liable to distract them and possibly set off the chase instinct if they are off leash.

## Tibetan Spaniel

**Size:** Small, 10", 9–15#

**Color:** All colors

**Protection:** Alarm dog

**Energy:** Medium–high

**Life expectancy:** 12–15 yrs.

**Children:** Happy playmate with gentle ones

**Other animals:** Play well with even the largest

**Abilities:** Agility, Obedience

**Shedding/Grooming:** Seasonal / Mist with water, use pin brush

**Health clearances:** OFA, CERF; **Ask about:** PRA, microphthalmia, patellar luxation

**Best with:** Social owners, participation in all activities

***Not for:*** Harsh handling, outdoor living

Tibetans have sporadic outbursts of energy, leaping and bounding, racing "like a car on a speedway," followed by curling up in a loved one's lap. They're often found "patrolling the perimeters of overstuffed armchairs or sofas, affording an eagle's-eye view through the windows." The Tibbie warns, then settles down in the nearest chair confident that all is in good hands.

These dogs greet most people with a happy wag and never forget a friend. They're easy care until spring, when they "leave a trail of soft wispy hair wherever they go and (finally) appear in their birthday suits."

## Tibetan Terrier

**Size:** Medium–small, 14–17", 18–30#

**Color:** Any color

**Protection:** Moderate, will bark

**Energy:** Moderate as puppies, low–moderate as adult

**Life expectancy:** 12–15 yrs.

**Children:** Yes, with civilized ones

**Other animals:** With those that accept them as alpha

**Abilities:** Obedience, Agility

**Shedding/Grooming:** Sheds within the coat, minimal on floor / Intensive during adolescence, easier in puppies and adults

**Health clearances:** OFA, CERF; **Ask about:** Patellar luxation, PRA, lens luxation, cataracts, hypothyroidism, vWD

**Best with:** Regular grooming, human companionship

***Not for:*** Outdoor living, families with small children

Persistence describes Tibetan problem solving, such as how to retrieve the toy from under the sofa. They're resourceful, like the one that pulls open cupboard doors and takes out cans of food to crush and pop, sucking out the food. Another uses his paws to open the refrigerator.

Tibetans like to have a reminder of their human around and sometimes pull clothes out of the laundry basket to sleep on when the person isn't home. These dogs learn quickly, then decide for themselves whether they'll remember at the appropriate time. They need an owner equal to the task of maintaining control.

# Herding Breeds

# 9 Round Up (Herding Breeds)

Shepherds and ranchers lead solitary lives, one reason they have dogs to keep them company. The other is they'd have to be marathon athletes to keep livestock together without a canine assistant.

Herding dogs, like many other hard-working canines, originally were bred for instinct and decision-making capabilities. Eventually, however, shepherds found one type better able to handle a certain kind of job, so owners began to focus on the diversity of the breeds, rather than blends. Shetland Sheepdogs fit perfectly in the tiny Shetland Islands and don't intimidate the miniature sheep and horses. Low-built Corgis dart under flying hooves and back out before cattle have a chance to retaliate. German Shepherd Dogs serve a dual purpose, protecting as well as herding the flocks. Australian Cattle Dogs are tough enough to withstand wild steers, long stock drives and the heat of the outback.

Many dogs lived with the sheep or did double duty at night keeping wild animals and ruffians from their masters' doors. Confidence and courage are common characteristics of most Herding dogs.They can find their way down a cliff to rescue a stray, now and then disobeying a command in order to protect a newborn lamb. Their protective instinct and independent thinking make them ideal for service-affiliated duties today. German Shepherds and Belgian Malinois are particularly sought after as police, military, and assistance dogs as well as aiding search and rescue. They're not the choice for someone who wants mindless obedience. Shepherds, Bouviers des Flandres, Briards and even the Old English Sheepdog served as guardians as well as herders. Early socialization and training helps keep them from becoming overprotective and to recognize their owner as the leader. The Border Collie's hypnotic stare directs the flocks. Others bark to warn intruders, scold a recalcitrant ram or "talk" a lazy sheep to its feet.

Although herders are willing playmates, they're content with indoor life. They bond closely to their people, need socialization and crave human contact.

**General characteristics:** Peppy, loyal, problem-solvers, territorial, content with adequate instinct outlet, strong chase instinct.

Bark: strong, businesslike bark.

## Australian Cattle Dog

**Size:** Medium, F. 17–19"; M. 18–20"

**Color:** Blue, blue mottled, red speckled

**Protection:** Very high; perceived intruders, such as FedEx courier, might be confined to the vehicle

**Energy:** Very high until age of five or six

**Life expectancy:** 10 yrs.

**Children:** If raised with them; driving instinct might transfer to kids, particularly those running and screaming

**Other animals:** Dominant; accept amiable dogs, preferably of opposite sex

**Abilities:** Herding, Obedience, Agility, Flyball

**Shedding/Grooming:** Yes, BIG time seasonally / Daily brushing

**Health clearances:** OFA, CERF, BAER; **Ask about:** OCD, PRA, glaucoma, lens luxation, deafness

**Best with:** Instinct outlet; confident, alpha, active owners; early, continuous socialization and Obedience training

***Not for:*** Apartments, submissive people, first-time owners, children under five years, sedentary life

The Cattle Dog from Down Under does everything full force. Also known as the Blue Heeler or Queensland Heeler, these dogs are strong-willed and confident, needing take-charge owners. The offensive lineman of the canine world, the Cattle Dog, at about the time of puberty, might challenge other dogs and people. Out-of-control Australian Cattle Dogs are capable of destroying a happy home and doing damage to themselves and others.

They're versatile enough for whatever activity people want to tackle: jogging, driving the cows or playing in any weather. Any dog that can be kicked in the head by a range steer and come back for more must be tough and courageous and cannot be forced into submission. This breed must be outsmarted and convinced your wish is theirs. When they give their hearts, they give all. Once they accept someone, they'll wiggle, leap, wag and bark in joyous greeting.

## Australian Shepherd

**Size:** Medium, 18–23", 45–65#

**Color:** Blue, red or liver merle, black or red with copper or tan tricolor

**Protection:** Strong

**Energy:** Medium–high

**Life expectancy:** 12–14 yrs.

**Children:** When socialized early; Intense herding instinct to gather

**Other animals:** Herd and boss others, but generally mix well

**Abilities:** Herding, Obedience, Agility, Flyball, search and rescue, Tracking

**Shedding/Grooming:** Heavy seasonal / Weekly brushing and combing, particularly during shed

**Health clearances:** OFA, CERF; **Ask about:** PRA, Collie Eye Anomaly, cataracts, glaucoma, microphthalmia, epilepsy

**Best with:** Active owners, fenced yards, early Obedience training, daily chores or job

***Not for:*** Backyard dogs, the sedentary, apartments

Reserved with strangers, the Aussie is mostly a one-family dog. If an owner says someone's okay, the dog will accept the person, but continue to watch that this stranger doesn't try to pocket the silverware or hurt the family.

A fast-moving, quick-thinking Aussie at work is a pleasure to see. Able to think out problems, these dogs are attentive, enthusiastic and easily trained. They aren't likely to be content fetching the paper unless owners receive two a day, plus mail, and the trek is a mile from the house. Buyers should search out fanciers who safeguard the breed's attributes and did not just jump on the popularity wagon.

## Bearded Collie

**Size:** Medium, F. 20–21", 40–45#; M. 21–22", 50–60#

**Color:** Black, brown, blue or fawn, usually with white markings

**Protection:** HA! On scale of 1–10, a .5; will bark (because they think the person has come to play with them)

**Energy:** Medium–high

**Life expectancy:** 12–14 yrs.

**Children:** Bouncy, playful, can be too exuberant for timid tots; might try to herd

**Other animals:** Accepting, but can be bossy over a coveted toy

**Abilities:** Herding, Obedience, Agility, therapy

**Shedding/Grooming:** Minimal / About 1 hr. weekly brushing and combing, NO trimming; will mat with neglect

**Health clearances:** OFA; **Ask about:** Cataracts, Addison's Disease, hypothyroidism, autoimmune diseases

**Best with:** Intense family bonding, activities, regular grooming, sense of humor

***Not for:*** Backyard dogs, perfectionists, robotic Obedience

Social dogs, Beardies are never happier than when in the midst of things. Yet, after a rowdy play session, they're content to lie at your feet. They're *not* protective; it's "Steal the house, steal me, that's okay." Owners need to be quicker-thinking than the Beardie, not always easy. One decided to satisfy his curiosity during a scent retrieve by searching through the judge's purse.

Finding a breeder who is expecting a litter takes time and persistence. Owners find their capricious charisma, curiosity and changing coat colors intriguing. "The Beardie is like a canine unicorn, a living, breathing, whimsical fairy-tale creature."

## Belgian Malinois

**Size:** Medium–large, F. 22–24", 50–60#; M. 24–26", 55–75#

**Color:** Fawn to mahogany, with black mask and ears

**Protection:** High

**Energy:** High, a turn around the backyard won't do it

**Life expectancy:** 10–12 yrs.

**Children:** Good if raised with them

**Other animals:** Accept as long as can be leader

**Abilities:** Herding, Obedience, Tracking, service fields

**Shedding/Grooming:** Yes / Minimal

**Health clearances:** OFA, CERF;
**Ask about:** PRA, pannus, cataracts, epilepsy, hypothyroidism

**Best with:** Interaction, early training/socialization, exercise

***Not for:*** Inexperienced handlers, busy households

The Malinois has become a breed of choice for law enforcement work and search and rescue. Malinois have a high degree of trainability, stamina and dedication to their jobs. Loyal to a handler, Mals will follow directions, but use their own talented senses as well.

Ignore Mals or leave them to their own devices, and personality quirks can develop. Choose lines carefully to avoid fearfulness. Take this dog to a class, show off abilities at a demonstration, utilize natural intelligence, and it'll pay off threefold. Powerful and agile, the Mal can outmuscle most people, so handlers need to establish control by giving strong, clear messages.

## Belgian Sheepdog

Photo: Downey

**Size:** Medium–large, F. 22–24", 40–60#; M. 25–26", 50–75#

**Color:** Black

**Protection:** High, good watchdogs

**Energy:** High

**Life expectancy:** 10–12 yrs.

**Children:** When raised with them

**Other animals:** Strong chase instinct

**Abilities:** Herding, Obedience, Agility, therapy

**Shedding/Grooming:** Yes! Everywhere, dog hair! / Weekly pin brushing; mist with water first

**Health clearances:** OFA, CERF;
**Ask about:** PRA, cataracts, pannus, epilepsy, hypothyroidism

**Best with:** Early, regular training and socialization; interaction

***Not for:*** Ignoring, fastidious housekeepers, impatient owners, heavy-handed corrections, high heat

Belgians, a.k.a. Groenendals, prefer their own people to all others. Owners say they can't even go to the bathroom alone. The Belgian is often aloof with strangers. They should be confident, however, not shy. A dominant streak will be modified through early training. Belgians are versatile, capable of doing almost anything the owner wants. Some will kill small rodents trespassing in their yard. Indoors, they're graceful pets. Regular dental care helps avoid health problems.

## Belgian Tervuren

**Size:** Medium–large, F. 22–24", 45–60#; M. 24–26", 65–80#

**Color:** Fawn to mahogany, with black

**Protection:** High, but not aggressive

**Energy:** High

**Life expectancy:** 10–14 yrs.

**Children:** With considerate kids; can become too rambunctious when around excitable ones

**Other animals:** Tolerate when raised with them and taught boundaries; high prey instinct; many "see cats as squeaky toys … or dinner."

**Abilities:** Herding, Obedience, Agility, Tracking, Flyball, Scent Hurdles

**Shedding/Grooming:** Heavy seasonal shed / Weekly brushing, more during shed

**Health clearances:** OFA, CERF; **Ask about:** Elbow dysplasia, cataracts, epilepsy, hypothyroidism

**Best with:** Active confident owners, training, quality time, early socialization, daily interaction, frequent runs

***Not for:*** Small children, fastidious housekeepers, first-time owners

Eager workers, Tervurens can overdo it and become overheated in summer. They enjoy a challenge. Owners warn, "They're quick to pick up bad habits as well as good." If it comes under the category of "fun," they'll eagerly join in. Some participate in sledding as well as their other activities.

Very much one-family dogs, they are wary of strangers. Many owners state that Belgians are particularly naughty puppies and stress the necessity of crates until the age of eighteen months. It's suggested owners should take the dog "everywhere they would take their wallet or purse."

## Border Collie

**Size:** Medium, 18–20", 30–45#

**Color:** Black, blue, chocolate, red, with or without white markings or merling

**Protection:** Medium–high, wary of strangers

**Energy:** High

**Life expectancy:** 13 yrs.

**Children:** Will try to drive and control them

**Other animals:** Can be testy with other dogs

**Abilities:** Herding, Obedience, Tracking, Flyball, Agility, therapy

**Shedding/Grooming:** Minimal

**Health clearances:** OFA, CERF, BAER; **Ask about:** OCD, PRA and other eye problems, deafness, epilepsy, paralysis

**Best with:** Lots of exercise, a job to do, Obedience

***Not for:*** Inactive owners, boredom, small children

Border Collies are the consummate canine athletes. They'll accompany owners in any activity, particularly those that involve running. Awesome in Herding Trials, they possess a strong eye. Border Collies still number among the favorites as working dogs on farms and ranches. Swift, agile and dependable, this breed is an Obedience star. Unlike most dogs, they love repetition and precise regimentation. Their attitude is, "Oh, boy, this is the 405th time I've retrieved this glove. Let's see if I can do it better this time!"

They must be kept busy or are liable to invent their own fun, which isn't always appropriate for house dogs.

## Bouvier des Flandres

**Size:** Large, 65–130#, F. 23.5–26.5"; M. 24.5–27.5"

**Color:** Fawn to black, salt and pepper, gray, brindle

**Protection:** High, especially for loved ones

**Energy:** Medium–high

**Life expectancy:** 10–12 yrs.

**Children:** When raised with them, enjoys romping and playing; size and strength can be a problem

**Other animals:** Never confine with another of same sex

**Abilities:** Herding, Obedience, search and rescue, carting, service fields

**Shedding/Grooming:** Although not profuse, hair sticks to carpets (and contact lenses) like Velcro / Hand stripping or clipping for pets, with some scissoring, combing and brushing twice a week or "can look like an unmowed lawn if neglected"

**Health clearances:** OFA, CERF; **Ask about:** HD, cataracts, glaucoma, entropion, torsion, hypothyroidism, laryngeal paralysis, cancerous tumors

**Best with:** Early training; strong, confident owners; gentle but firm handling; roomy, fenced yard

***Not for:*** Timid people, lazy groomers, cramped quarters with no exercise, warm and humid climates

When given a signal that all is well, a Bouvier will relax but maintain watch, all the while tail-wagging. Bouvs can press for leadership if allowed. They hit puberty at full throttle. "Bouvs that have been perfect little angels throughout little-bearhood suddenly forget manners and turn into unruly devils. One leaped onto the table, splattering peas and potatoes skyward. He answered the telephone and eventually ate the receiver, and barked incessently when alone." Buyers need to be prepared, and it helps to have a sense of humor.

## Briard

Photo: B. Kernan

**Size:** Large, 65–85#, F. 22–25.5"; M. 23–27"

**Color:** Black, gray, tawny

**Protection:** Booming bark; threatening intruder in deep trouble—"they would die for one of their flock"

**Energy:** Adjusts to owner

**Life expectancy:** 10–12 yrs.

**Children:** If raised with them; sometimes protect charges from spanking

**Other animals:** Accept as part of flock; supervise introduction of new pets

**Abilities:** Herding

**Shedding/Grooming:** Yes / Brush adults weekly, puppies daily

**Health clearances:** OFA, CERF; **Ask about:** PRA, bloat, hypothyroidism

**Best with:** Firm, confident owners; early training and socialization

***Not for:*** Small children, pushovers

Briards take their jobs seriously and go all out in play. The drover instinct is high, and they will often bump people along. Some are jealous and must learn their place in the pack. Their memory is elephantine and they'll remember an unfair correction.

These dogs learn quickly and like to put newfound talent to work rather than performing by rote. Instead of having them fetch a dumbbell 100 times, do it three or four times, then switch to bringing the paper in or carrying slippers upstairs. Finish with a few more tosses of the dumbbell, and they'll be more cooperative trainees.

## Collie (Rough and Smooth)

**Size:** Medium–large, F. 22–24", 50–65#; M. 24–26", 60–75#

**Color:** Sable and white, tricolor, blue merle, white

**Protection:** Low, a bark and a wag

**Energy:** Medium

**Life expectancy:** 12 yrs.

**Children:** Excellent

**Other animals:** Usually very good

**Abilities:** Herding, Obedience, Agility, therapy

**Shedding/Grooming:** Seasonal / Weekly brushing

**Health clearances:** OFA, CERF; **Ask about:** PRA, Collie Eye Anomaly and other eye problems, deafness, hypothyroidism, PDA

**Best with:** Close bonding to family

***Not for:*** Ignoring, protection, harsh handling

Every child's dream of a loving, heroic, furry pal, this breed craves human companionship. When left alone, a Collie will voice displeasure, which can prove maddening to those within hearing distance. Collies are dependable workers and will almost turn themselves inside out to please. They wag their enjoyment as much on the 800th command as they do the first.

Those who are looking for a "Lassie" or "Lad," that leaps into burning buildings and swims roaring rivers—or even one that collects eggs, meets the school bus and pulls kids in a cart—may be disappointed. All these attributes take time and patience to teach. If a sweet, affectionate companion is the desire, Collies delight owners.

## German Shepherd Dog

**Size:** Large, F. 22–24", 60–70#; M. 24–26", 75–95#

**Color:** Black and tan, sable, black

**Protection:** High, will not back down if owner or property threatened

**Energy:** Moderate, good stamina

**Life expectancy:** 12 yrs.

**Children:** Excellent from well-bred lines

**Other animals:** Most are tolerant

**Abilities:** Herding, Obedience, search and rescue, service fields

**Shedding/Grooming:** OH, YES! Wall-to-wall hair / Brush, brush, brush; use rake and comb during shed

**Health clearances:** OFA hips and elbows, CERF; **Ask about:** OCD, bloat, torsion, spinal disease, epilepsy, pancreatitis, perianal fistulas, HD*

**Best with:** Fenced yards, Obedience, close human contact, industrial-strength vacuum

***Not for:*** Isolation, robotic Obedience, inactive people

It's said many breeds can do a specific job better, but none can do so many as well as the German Shepherd Dog. The breed's rise and fall in popularity has brought concurrent health and temperament problems. Buyers are cautioned to demand soundness and health clearances. A large dangerous dog can be more lethal than a little one.

A well-bred Shepherd is a combination of power, nobility and agility. Admirers feel this breed's regal carriage gives them "the look of eagles." German Shepherds are undemanding, yet ready to participate in any activity when invited. Owners say, "I can look in my Shepherd's eyes and know he will die for me."

## Old English Sheepdog

Photo: A. Smith

**Size:** Large, 70–100#, F. 21"+; M. 22"+

**Color:** Gray, grizzle, blue, blue merle, with or without white

**Protection:** Low; assists burglar in carrying valuables to the door, but has BOOMING bark

**Energy:** Low as adults

**Life expectancy:** 12–13 yrs.

**Children:** Outstanding; may nip at the heels of running, playing kids; may be too rambunctious for small kids

**Other animals:** Enjoy the company of others; females tend to be more bossy

**Abilities:** Herding, Obedience, Flyball

**Shedding/Grooming:** Little when properly groomed / High maintenance or high expense, six to eight hours per week; some pets clipped

**Health clearances** OFA, CERF; **Ask about:** PRA and other eye problems, diabetes, deafness, hypothyroidism, wobblers

**Best with:** Confident owners, wannabe hairdressers

***Not for:*** Lazy groomers, overly busy people, fussy housekeepers

The OES looks like a lovable, shaggy clown. And that's what they are best at. A poorly bred one can be impatient with children and confuse the mail carrier with a mass murderer. Sheepdogs can be hard-headed, but if you're willing to work around their agenda, everything's cool.

They need exercise to keep in good shape, but this doesn't occur simply by turning them out in the yard. They lie by the back door waiting for you to come out and play. They're crowd pleasers in competition and scent hurdle races when owners have the patience to persist. At home, they are a three-ring circus for their owners' pleasure.

## Puli

Photo: Wacker

**Size:** Medium, 30–35#, F. 16", M. 17"

**Color:** Rusty black, black, gray, white

**Protection:** Will bark, often suspicious of strangers

**Energy:** High

**Life expectancy:** 14–16 yrs.

**Children:** If raised with them, better with older ones; often bump them along with nose

**Other animals:** Will herd

**Abilities:** Herding, Obedience, Agility

**Shedding/Grooming:** Not noticeable, sheds within coat / Specialized cording or extensive brushing, mats if neglected

**Health clearances:** OFA, CERF; **Ask about:** PRA, cataracts

**Best with:** Firm, fair training; active owners who like to work with dogs

***Not for:*** Wash-and-wear care, fading into the wallpaper

The Puli's natural springy gait shows its joy of life. With more bounce to the ounce, their high jumps might land them on the backs of sheep—or furniture. Barking comes naturally, so owners must teach the dog to be selective about sounding an alarm.

As a Puli grows into maturity, cords must be separated into *neat* dreadlocks. Bathing and drying require nearly a day. With the upturned tail and the cords falling over the eyes, it's hard to tell whether the dog is coming or going. He needs to be cleaned frequently fore and aft, or the remnants of dinner entering and leaving will leave an odor.

## Shetland Sheepdog

Photo: J. Haederlie

**Size:** Small–medium, 13–16"

**Color:** Black, tricolor, blue merle and sable, with white or tan markings

**Protection:** Moderate, will bark

**Energy:** Medium–high

**Life expectancy:** 12–14 yrs.

**Children:** Find kids companionable; rowdy youngsters too much for these gentle souls

**Other animals:** Sociable

**Abilities:** Herding, Obedience, Agility

**Shedding/Grooming:** Yes / Brush weekly, more during shed

**Health clearances:** OFA, CERF; **Ask about:** Legg-Perthes, patellar luxation, PRA, cataracts, Collie Eye Anomaly, PDA, hypothyroidism, epilepsy

**Best with:** Puppy kindergarten, gentle commands

***Not for:*** Harsh commands, roughhousing, backyard dogs

Shetland Sheepdogs are sensitive and in tune to their owners. They learn quickly and are eager to please, attentive with speedy response to commands. Intently listening to owners' every word, they seem to understand. Nevertheless, they need to be subtly taught who is the pack leader.

Although sometimes called a miniature Collie, the Sheltie is more reserved or even timid with new people or situations. These dogs startle easily and don't like to be teased. When excited or lonely, Shelties can be barky. Buyers might find a delightful specimen a mite too big or small for the show ring, but just right for their arms.

## Cardigan Welsh Corgi

Photo: Attic Studio

**Size:** Small–medium, 10.5–12.5", F. 25–35#; M. 30–40#

**Color:** Red, sable, brindle, black or merle; may have brindling, tan points and/or white markings

**Protection:** Will sound a warning

**Energy:** Medium–high, but not hyper

**Life expectancy:** 12 yrs.

**Children:** Yes, if raised with them; will herd

**Other animals:** Don't recognize they're vertically challenged; will not back down from much larger dogs

**Abilities:** Herding, Tracking, Obedience, Agility

**Shedding/Grooming:** Seasonally heavy / Weekly brushing; comb, comb, comb during shed

**Health clearances:** OFA, CERF; **Ask about:** PRA and other eye problems, intervertebral disk disease, vWD

**Best with:** Fenced yards, a sense of humor

***Not for:*** Outside life; the houseproud; a quiet, dull life

The long-tailed Cardigan tends to be more laid back than the Pembroke. Cardis have a big dog's body on short legs. Reserved with strangers, this breed prefers to make the first overture. They tend to be vocal about differences of opinion or a change in the weather and occasionally seem to hum a chorus of "Cow Cow Boogie."

Owners say barring pearl diving, Cardigans tackle almost any other activity. Tough and low enough to dodge kicks, they handle cattle without ruffling a hair. Bred to drive recalcitrant steers by nipping at their heels, Cardis will sometimes transfer this tactic to equally stubborn humans.

## Pembroke Welsh Corgi

**Size:** Small, 10–12", 25–30#

**Color:** Red, sable, fawn, black and tan; may have white markings

**Protection:** Will bark

**Energy:** Moderate

**Life expectancy:** 13–14 yrs.

**Children:** Usually good

**Other animals:** Prefer to lead rather than follow

**Abilities:** Obedience, Herding, Tracking

**Shedding/Grooming:** Seasonal, profuse / Brushing and combing

**Health clearances:** OFA, CERF; **Ask about:** PRA and other eye problems, intervertebral disk disease, cystinuria, vWD

**Best with:** Quality time, Obedience

***Not for:*** Spoiling, long hours alone, an ornament

A tad smaller than the Cardigan, Pembrokes like to know who is going to run the household. If no one speaks up, the Pem will take charge. They can be manipulative in achieving their own way. Invited to do any type of activity, the Corgis are enthusiastic. Yet they're content to join the family for channel surfing after a busy day.

Many owners of other Herding dogs choose the Pembroke Corgi for a second breed, because they have a big-dog heart in a compact body. It's important to watch the waistlines of both Corgi breeds. Extra poundage puts stress on the long back, increasing the chance of disk and joint problems.

# Miscellaneous and Rare Breeds

# 10

# Et Cetera (Miscellaneous and Rare Breeds)

Several of these breeds are in the AKC **Miscellaneous** Group. Some breeds are populous and easily found. Others are rare and currently seeking AKC Miscellaneous status. A few are striving to remain independent organizations. Many are recognized by various other kennel clubs around the world. As more breeds become approved, they will enter their appropriate classification. But, of course, they already fit the characteristics of their future groups.

Lesser-known breeds may have fewer health problems than popular ones, primarily because many of these breeds do not exist in sufficient numbers to have particular problems show up repeatedly. It is usually the case that when any breed is populous enough for problems to recur, breeders begin testing. It is only with testing that patterns can be established for medical abnormalities. Some, in fact, have not listed any significant defects. Still, it's wise to ask, "Does this breed have problems I should be aware of?" Request references of former buyers.

Of course, there is also the fun of owning something different. Most of these dogs are close to their origins, both in temperament and physique.

Photo: Garden Studio

## Anatolian Shepherd Dog

**Size:** Giant, F. 28–31", 88–121#; M. 29–32", 110–143#

**Color:** Fawn, brindle, tricolor, white, black, black mask

**Protection:** Very high

**Energy:** Low, except when threat is perceived; calm, laid-back house pets

**Life expectancy:** 10–15 yrs.

**Children:** Generally, can misread parental correction or rough play as threat

**Other animals:** Family pets accepted as flock, unfamiliar animals considered trespassers; males not tolerant of others

**Abilities:** Weight Pulling, Obedience

**Shedding/Grooming:** Seasonal heavy shed / Brushing

**Health clearances:** OFA hips and elbows; **Ask about:** Entropion, hypothyroidism

**Best with:** A job, training, high fencing, early socialization

***Not for:*** Competitive Obedience; off-leash walks; yard-proud, submissive or frail people

Happiest patrolling livestock, the Anatolian's *modus operandi* is to warn with barking and a threatening appearance. If necessary, however, these dogs are strong and agile enough to overtake and thwart a predator, animal or human. When raised in suburbia, these canine guards need confinement, or they will usurp neighbors' property to protect—perhaps from the neighbors themselves! These dogs are known to dig and occasionally to scale fences. They aren't content without a job, even if it's "Bring me the remote control, Zorba." Anatolians are stoic and should be examined regularly for any injuries or sores they haven't complained about.

If owners do not take charge during puppyhood, the Anatolian will. Many challenge the leader during puberty. Dominance games such as tug-of-war or tag should be avoided. Instead use command-and-reward play, such as "Get the ball," "Lie down," "Come," followed by lots of praise.

## Argentine Dogo

Photo: B. Harkins

**Size:** Large, 80–100#, F. 24.5–27", M. 24.5–27"

**Color:** White

**Protection:** High

**Energy:** High; exuberant outdoors, calm indoors

**Life expectancy:** 10–12 yrs.

**Children:** When raised with them

**Other animals:** Most accept household pets when raised with them; use judgment in introducing new animals

**Abilities:** Hunting big game, Obedience, Tracking, service fields

**Shedding/Grooming:** Minimal / Minimal; prevent pressure point sores and calluses with foam cushions

**Health clearances:** OFA, BAER, **Ask about:** Deafness

**Best with:** Fence; strong, confident owners

***Not for:*** Elderly, inactive people, first-time owners, easily dominated

Dogos can be determined to follow their own course. It takes knowledge and resources on the part of owners to maintain control. At home, the Dogo personality is much like a Boxer's in a stronger body. Visitors can be intimidated when a 100-pound animal's teeth are at eye level, however, even if they're hidden by a welcoming slurp.

## Australian Kelpie

**Size:** Medium, F. 17–20"; M. 20–23"

**Color:** Black, red, cream, fawn, chocolate, blue, with or without tan markings

**Protection:** Will bark

**Energy:** Inexhaustibly high!!!—if Greyhounds are canine equivalent of Olympian sprinters, Kelpies are marathoners

**Life expectancy:** 10–14 yrs.

**Children:** Good when raised with them; may herd and nip at heels

**Other animals:** Herded whether they want to or not

**Abilities:** Herding, Herding, Herding, Obedience, Tracking, service fields

**Shedding/Grooming:** Yes / Wash and wear

**Health clearances:** OFA, CERF; **Ask about:** OCD, PRA

**Best with:** A job, room to exercise, high fences or roofed kennel run on cement surface

***Not for:*** The sedentary, city living, lapdog or a docile pet

These workaholics "will work until they drop. They are independent and in business for themselves rather than pleasing a handler." Boredom is the breed's nemesis and owners' as well. In their native country, Kelpies work all day even in intense heat, covering 1,000 to 4,000-plus acres. The breed uses "eye" similar to the Border Collie's on tractable stock, but utilizes its nipping ability to turn more obstinate cattle.

Kelpies muster sheep in thousands from pasture to pen to truck. When a flock of sheep is packed as tight as Times Square on New Year's Eve, the shortest way from one point to another is a straight line. The clever Kelpie has figured a way to reach the other side of the flock: It jumps on the back of the nearest sheep and runs lightly across the flock. Kelpie owners are more interested in working ability than in progressing to Championship status.

## Beauceron

**Size:** Large, F. 24–26.75"; M. 25.5–27.5"

**Color:** Black and tan, harlequin (gray, black and tan tricolor)

**Protection:** High; diligent, alert and confident

**Energy:** Medium

**Life expectancy:** 10–12 yrs.

**Children:** When raised with them; rowdy, large puppy may be too exuberant for small child

**Other animals:** Usually good with household pets when raised with them; will send signals to trespasser that he'd better find another tree to mark

**Abilities:** Obedience, Tracking, Agility, Herding, search and rescue, flock guardian, service fields

**Shedding/Grooming:** Minimal / Brush

**Health clearances/Ask about:** OFA

**Best with:** Confident owners, training, a job, frequent people contact

***Not for:*** Small children, inactive people

Beaucerons are calm, dependable and eager to learn, carrying out commands with finesse. They're comparable to German Shepherd Dogs in utility, possessing the grace and smooth lines of the Doberman Pinscher.

Within the perimeters of family dog, the Beauce tempers guarding instincts but always remains observant. Good-natured with all family members, one will usually be a favorite. Beaucerons have respect for the person who takes time to train and work them.

## Canaan Dog

**Size:** Medium, 19–24", F. 35#; M. 50–55#

**Color:** White with black, brown or red markings; brown or black, with or without white markings

**Protection:** Alert and wary of strangers, will sound alarm

**Energy:** Moderate

**Life expectancy:** 13–15 yrs.

**Children:** When raised with them

**Other animals:** Accept as part of pack; sometimes sharp with other dogs

**Abilities:** Obedience, Tracking, search and rescue, Herding

**Shedding/Grooming:** Constant minimal shed, more seasonally / Brush

**Health clearances:** OFA, CERF; **Ask about:** PRA

**Best with:** Secure fencing, early socialization, people contact

***Not for:*** Perfection Obedience, wagging acceptance of all, those who don't appreciate self-thinkers

Slow to warm to visitors, Canaans prefer to do so at their own pace. Like Terriers, this breed will dispatch vermin. Observant of all around them, Canaans become distracted easily. They are willing to please, however, and learn house manners easily.

This resourceful dog survived for many years as a resident of the desert, fending for itself, giving the breed a high instinct for self-preservation. Totally natural, Canaans have not been molded artificially.

## Dogue de Bordeaux

**Size:** Large, F. 23–25", 100–130#; M. 25–27", 120–150#

**Color:** Dark auburn or fawn; may have white on chest

**Protection:** Very high; tough mug, powerful body and booming bark keep intruders at bay

**Energy:** Medium–high

**Life expectancy:** 8–12 yrs.

**Children:** Yes

**Other animals:** Dominant; familiar dogs are accepted, strange ones are not

**Abilities:** Obedience

**Shedding/Grooming:** Seasonal / Brush

**Health clearances:** OFA; **Ask about:** Cancer

**Best with:** Early socialization and training; strong, confident owner

***Not for:*** Easily dominated, fastidious, hot and humid weather

Despite the breed's bulk, the Dogue de Bordeaux is muscular and athletic, and some owners jog with their canine bodyguard. With adequate exercise on leash, the breed even adapts to apartment living.

Fanciers say the dog is careful with the smallest child. They are content with a human in charge. One of the biggest problems is the breed's desire to be a lap dog.

The DdB drools—a lot—in hot weather and appreciates air-conditioning.

## German Pinscher

**Size:** Medium, 17–20", 25–35#

**Color:** Black and tan, red

**Protection:** High, capable of stopping intruder if pressed

**Energy:** High

**Life expectancy:** 12–13 yrs.

**Children:** Can be difficult for kids to control

**Other animals:** If socialized early or raised with them

**Abilities:** Obedience

**Shedding/Grooming:** Minimal / Minimal

**Health clearances:** OFA, CERF; **Ask about:** Eye problems

**Best with:** Active owners, lots of exercise, early socialization and training

***Not for:*** Easily dominated or overly busy people, outdoor living

This breed is described as feisty, alert, sturdy and active. With a terrier background, the German Pinscher finishes off rodents with a shake of the head. If not given adequate exercise and access to a fenced yard, they make do within four walls, bouncing off them or setting up a canine racetrack. German Pinschers need to be reminded of who's boss. They can be manipulative and will try to get their way if possible. When handled by a knowledgeable trainer, they can excel in Obedience.

## Havanese

*Photo: DiGiacomo*

**Size:** Small, 8.5–11.5", 7–13#

**Color:** Coats of many colors

**Protection:** Will alert; "courageous and fearless in the face of danger"

**Energy:** Medium

**Life expectancy:** 12–15 yrs.

**Children:** Adore little people and will play games for hours

**Other animals:** Greeted with glee

**Abilities:** Obedience, therapy

**Shedding/Grooming:** Shed *within* coat / Brush every other day or will mat; some pets clipped, especially around eyes

**Health clearances:** CERF, palpation for patellar luxation; **Ask about:** Cataracts, hypothyroidism, knee (patella) problems

**Best with:** Gentle handling, playful owners, regular grooming

***Not for:*** Ignoring, rough children

The Havanese is a charming, open-hearted breed with a spirit of cooperation. They're soft-natured and their feelings can be hurt. "Havanese learn quickly who is in charge and rarely challenge for dominance."

Those fancying the Havanese can choose from curly or wavy coats. An owner stresses, "There's a real dog under all that hair." It's an ideal choice for some one who wants a small, sweet-tempered dog that's not fragile or yappy. Knee palpation attested to with a veterinary signature is required by the Parent Club in order to register pups.

## Irish Red and White Setter

**Size:** Medium–large, F. 22–23"; M. 24–25"

**Color:** White with red

**Protection:** Nil, but will bark; wary of strangers

**Energy:** High; exuberant as youngsters, become more sedate with maturity

**Life expectancy:** 12–14 yrs.

**Children:** Yes, with supervision to control puppy enthusiasm

**Other animals:** Enjoy family dogs, but bred to run and will chase cats

**Abilities:** Upland bird dog and retriever, Obedience

**Shedding/Grooming:** Minimal / Minimal brushing

**Health clearances:** OFA, CERF; **Ask about:** Cataracts

**Best with:** Active owners, hunters, exercise, interaction, runners, socialization

***Not for:*** Sit-at-homes, the elderly, harsh methods

Many Red and White Setters prefer to make their own approach. "Teens" occasionally go through a timid period. These setters have soft dispositions. They're always alert and observant, with ears and eyes moving—nerve-wracking for the Obedience competitor.

Extremely people-oriented, they can be clingy. Red and Whites often grin at their owners and talk. These dogs want to please, but are prone to dreaming up their own entertainment if left to themselves for very long. They might become interior decorators and renovate the furniture, for instance. Owners note their urge to be in high places: on top of crates, chairs, people. Some walk on top of fences and climb or jump even six-foot enclosures.

## Italian Spinoni

**Size:** Large, F. 22.5–25.5", 70–80#; M. 23.5–27.5", 80–90#

**Color:** White; may have orange or chestnut markings or roaning

**Protection:** Will bark; size a deterrent

**Energy:** Moderate

**Life expectancy:** 13–14 yrs.

**Children:** Patient; adore children, seek their company

**Other animals:** Sociability carries over to all

**Abilities:** Hunting and retrieving upland and water birds, Obedience, Tracking, Field Trials, Hunting Tests

**Shedding/Grooming:** Minimal / Brush, some stripping to neaten; frequently clean large, floppy ears

**Health clearances:** OFA;
**Ask about:** Bloat

**Best with:** Hunters, athletes, fenced yard

***Not for:*** Isolation, idleness

Not as wound up as many Sporting dogs, Spinoni will reside contentedly in condos with access to daily runs. They are often cautious about new people and situations. Spinoni manage to tuck their girth into cramped spaces in order to accompany their people. One owner takes "eight or nine in my small station wagon!"

Hunters note the dog is always under control, working easily within gun range. Nevertheless, the breed is an eager hunter, vigorous and hardy, searching in heavy cover and diving into icy waters to retrieve. They need little correction, always keeping an eye on the hunter, "hunting for their master, rather than themselves."

## Jack Russell Terrier

**Size:** Small, 12–15", 11–16#

**Color:** White with brown, black or tricolor markings

**Protection:** Will bark

**Energy:** High

**Life expectancy:** 14–16 yrs.

**Children:** Very good with well-behaved ones, but assertive; will not tolerate poking and prodding

**Other animals:** Dog-aggressive, willing to take on Rottweilers; cats or small pets are endangered species; horse is only tolerable four-footed companion

**Abilities:** Hunting below/above ground, Agility, Obedience

**Shedding/Grooming:** Yes / Brushing

**Health clearances:** OFA, CERF;
**Ask about:** Legg-Perthes, patellar luxation, ataxia, eye problems. The Jack Russell club does not register inbred dogs or those with genetic faults. Dogs must be one year old and have medical report.

**Best with:** Active, quick-minded owners, patient trainers, fenced yard, small-game hunters

***Not for:*** Status symbol, small or rough children, apartment living

The Jack Russell Terrier is active, inquisitive and cheerful. Feisty and able to tackle foxes, raccoons or woodchucks, they've proven themselves valuable to farmers or home owners plagued with rodents. These game little dogs dig tunnels in pursuit of a varmint, staying underground for hours or even days, in a face-off with the inhabitant. JRs are tenacious, barking vermin to distraction. The wrong owner can be driven to the brink as well.

These dogs will take off in a flash and hunt 'til doomsday, which can come too soon if they're allowed to escape. JRs can be comical, while frustrating, climbing on top of bookshelves, into cupboards and drawers and through almost anything. They gamely kill socks or ferocious squeaky toys. Most fanciers oppose Kennel Club recognition.

## Lowchen

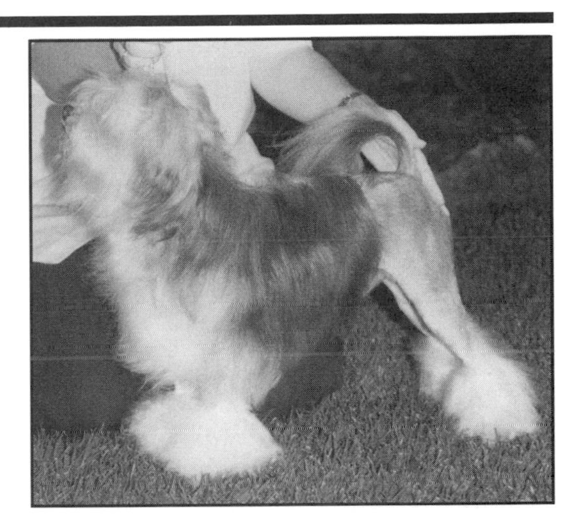

**Size:** Small, 12–14", 12–18#

**Color:** Any color

**Protection:** Will alert

**Energy:** Moderate

**Life expectancy:** 14–16 yrs.

**Children:** Gentle with well-trained youngsters.

**Other animals:** Friendly

**Abilities:** Obedience, therapy

**Shedding/Grooming:** Shed into coat / Brushing, tangles if neglected; clip for showing

**Health clearances:** OFA, CERF; **Ask about:** Patellar luxation, PRA, cataracts

**Best with:** Lots of attention

***Not for:*** People who are seldom home, outdoor living

Although Lowchen are spunky and high-spirited, they're also happy to curl up in a lap. They have a good attention span and long memory, making them a joy to work in Obedience or simply to teach good manners.

The Lowchen is shown with a lion clip, reminiscent of the Portuguese Water Dog or Poodle. Leonine cut aside, Lowchens reign as kings of hearts rather than the jungle. They make good apartment dogs, compact and easygoing.

## Neapolitan Mastiff

**Size:** Giant, F. 23–27.5", 110–132#; M. 25–30", 132–154#

**Color:** Gray, blue, black, mahogany, tawny, with or without brindling

**Protection:** Courageous guardian; wary and distrusting of strangers, but discriminating and not quick-tempered

**Energy:** Low, except when provoked

**Life expectancy:** 8–9 yrs.

**Children:** When raised with them and well socialized

**Other animals:** Okay with dogs of opposite sex; accept and guard other family pets and livestock; introduce with caution—"not apt to instigate a battle, but few will back down if challenged."

**Abilities:** Tracking, Obedience, Weight Pulling, draft dogs

**Shedding/Grooming:** Minimal / Brush; clean ears frequently

**Health clearances:** OFA; **Ask about:** HD, elbow dysplasia, OCD, hypothyroidism, heart problems, entropion, bloat

**Best with:** Strong and confident owners, early socialization, control training, fenced yard

***Not for:*** Apartments, the frail or elderly, heat and humidity, first-time owners, small children, the houseproud

Not just another pretty face, the Neapolitan Mastiff is distinguished and rugged. Relaxed and quiet, the Neo is gentle with loved ones. These massive animals are intimidating to anyone foolish enough to test them. Fanciers warn against encouraging aggressive behavior with dominance games, such as tug-of-war or wrestling. They're expensive to buy, feed and transport (no Volvos here).

Neapolitan Mastiffs dribble food and water from their jowls, flinging "goobers" with a shake of the head. Snoring is part of the package. They are stoic and should be examined often for sores or wounds. Running and jumping should be curtailed in puppyhood to allow young bones to grow properly. This breed often prefers one family member over others.

## Norwegian Buhund

**Size:** Medium, 16–18"

**Color:** Wheaten, black, wolf sable, with white markings and black mask

**Protection:** Medium–high, courageous enough to protect home front

**Energy:** Medium–high

**Life expectancy:** 15–20 yrs.

**Children:** Tops; may transfer herding instincts to gathering

**Other animals:** Usually social

**Abilities:** Herding, Obedience, Agility, service fields

**Shedding/Grooming:** Seasonal / Brush vigorously when shedding

**Health clearances:** OFA, CERF; **Ask about:** Eye problems

**Best with:** Fences, maximum playtime, Obedience, family bonding

***Not for:*** Sedentary people, isolation, wishy-washy owners

Buhunds carry enough Nordic independence to be content when left alone. But they have a desire to please, tending to be more tractable and trainable than other Spitz types. Friendly and curious, the Buhund is willing to try any activity, especially if exposed to new experiences early on. Buhunds vocally communicate their joy of life, as well as alarms. This is not the dog for someone who wants a silent benchwarmer.

## Plott Hound

**Size:** Medium–large, 24–26", 55–65#

**Color:** Brindle, blue; may have black saddle

**Protection:** "Hardly! But if one were ever to bite a person, it would be in child protection."

**Energy:** High

**Life expectancy:** 10–15 yrs.

**Children:** Great

**Other animals:** Mix well with domestic animals; as many as eight or ten hunt together with nary a cross word

**Abilities:** Hunting, hunting, and more hunting

**Shedding/Grooming:** Hardly noticeable / Brush

**Health clearances/Ask about:** None reported

**Best with:** Hunters, exercise, fenced yards

***Not for:*** Apartments, invalids, city living, Obedience

Loving and sweet to their family, "Plotts lick, lick, lick, wag, wag, wag." They're submissive to all humans and greet them with a happy howl. But Plotts are tenacious with wild game, scent-trailing raccoons, big cats and even black bears. "If they start a track, they'll end it with the animal in the tree."

These hounds bay while on the trail, changing voice when they have treed their quarry. They might also bay when the moon rises, and sometimes just for the joy of it.

## Polish Owczarek Nizinny

**Size:** Medium, 17–20", 30–50#

**Color:** Any color

**Protection:** Medium; suspicious of strangers and alerts

**Energy:** Medium–high

**Life expectancy:** 12–15 yrs.

**Children:** Excellent when raised with children

**Other animals:** Friendly, but hold their own if someone tries to knock them out from being Top Dog

**Abilities:** Herding, Obedience, Tracking, Agility, therapy

**Shedding/Grooming:** Sheds into coat / Weekly brushing and combing or will mat; no clipping

**Health clearances:** OFA, CERF; **Ask about:** PDA

**Best with:** Firm consistent owners, frequent grooming, socialization and training

***Not for:*** Elderly or frail, first-time dog owner, outside living

As a Working dog for many centuries, the PONS is happiest when given a job to do. This breed is lively and clever enough to work sheep alone. Although strong-willed, the dog has an excellent memory. Once convinced something is the right way and makes an owner happy, the PONS is dependable.

This cute shaggy dog doesn't grow into a cuddly stuffed lapwarmer. The PONS is muscular and agile—also curious and liable to find trouble if left alone.

## Tibetan Mastiff

**Size:** Large–giant, 25–32", 70–140#

**Color:** Black, black and tan, blue and tan, brown, grizzle, sable, cream

**Protection:** Highly territorial; formal introductions a must. "The amount of force used will be equal to that perpetrated by the intruder."

**Energy:** Low

**Life expectancy:** 14 yrs.

**Children:** Adoring, but may be overwhelming to small or unsure children; playmates' rowdiness could be mistaken for threat; parental supervision is a must

**Other animals:** Some same-sex dog aggression

**Abilities:** Flock guarding

**Shedding/Grooming:** Yes / Brush

**Health clearances:** OFA; **Ask about:** HOD, hypothyroidism

**Best with:** Early Obedience and socialization, owners with leadership skills, fenced yard, low protein diets

***Not for:*** Frail or elderly people, apartments, push-button Obedience, drop-in visitors

If raised in cramped quarters with close neighbors, this canine bodyguard is going to resort to excessive barking or overguarding. "It doesn't matter if Mrs. Smith has been invited in 50 times, on the 51st time she will have to pass inspection again." Owners recommend a minimum quarter acre of open space for the dog to reign over.

Tibetan Mastiffs take time to mull over whether anything else is worth doing and whether an owner really means it. They have slow metabolisms and are not food oriented, eating much less than other large breeds. Exceptionally clean, they'll choose the furthest place to eliminate. Although loving with their family, "this breed does not need to be validated constantly by humans to be happy."

## Treeing Walker Hound

**Size:** Medium, 23–25", 50–60#

**Color:** Tricolor, occasionally bicolor

**Protection:** Nonexistent

**Energy:** Very high

**Life expectancy:** 10–12 yrs.

**Children:** Excellent

**Other animals:** Grumble at dogs of the same gender

**Abilities:** Hunting big game

**Shedding/Grooming:** Not noticeable / Brush

**Health clearances/ Ask about:** None reported

**Best with:** High amounts of exercise, hunting

***Not for:*** Sedentary or frail owners, apartments

Walkers are loving creatures, but don't have the psyche to be content indoors or pampered lap dogs. "Walkers have a one-track mind. They're game crazy."

As hunters, Walkers concentrate on raccoon or opossum, but can branch out to bear or bobcat. The Walker's loud voice can be heard for miles on a hunt, or in frustration if not hunting. They seldom fail to tree quarry, making them one of the most popular hunting dogs in the United States.

## Xoloitzicuintli

**Size:** Toy <13", Miniature <18", Standard 18–23"

**Color:** Charcoal, slate, red-gray, liver or bronze; may have pink or brown spots

**Protection:** Alert and will bark

**Energy:** Medium–high

**Life expectancy:** 15–17 yrs.

**Children:** Affectionate with kind, gentle kids

**Other animals:** Friendly

**Abilities:** Obedience, Agility

**Shedding/Grooming:** No for hairless, minimal for coated / Daily wet wipe, followed by hand lotion; frequent bathing or pimples and blackheads erupt; occasional brushing for coated variety

**Health clearances:** None reported; **Ask about:** Skin problems

**Best with:** Frequent cleansing, plenty of affection

***Not for:*** Outdoor living, people who want silence, toys for children

The Xoloitzcuintli needs a coat or sweater for cold weather and sun screen in summer heat. With no hair, they're a possibility for dog-loving allergy sufferers.

The smallest Xolo is among the hardiest of Toy breeds. Reserved with visitors, Xolos make overtures after relaxing. Active and alert, but not nervous, this breed is attentive and will dote on your every word.

# Appendices

# Walkowicz's Words to the Wise

- *You* have to live with the dog.
- Thought beforehand will save later pain for both of you.
- The free (giveaway) dog is not always the most reasonable.
- Look at the mother and at least a photo of the father. Seeing both parents is okay if you are at a fair-sized, well-established kennel, *but* if the "breeder" only has the two animals and these are the parents of this (and perhaps *every*) litter, the breeders may have done what was easy, not necessarily what was best.
- Ask to see what health and/or genetic tests have been done on the parents.
- Do not act or react harshly.
- Papers do not necessarily mean registration papers, and registration papers do not necessarily mean quality.
- The most important time of a puppy's life is between eight and ten weeks.
- Puppies with manners are lifetime companions, not puppy delinquents.
- The key word in teaching is *praise.*
- Groom regularly for the health and comfort of the dog.
- Toys expand dogs' minds.

- Be tuned in to your pet.
- A confined (fenced, leashed) dog has a long life.
- The best insurances for your dog are a leash and a crate.
- Neutering is the best and simplest means of pet population control, as well as being healthier for your pets and making them more content.
- Sound parents make sound pups.
- Socialize, socialize, socialize.
- Obtain a contract and read it.
- Even if nobody in the world likes you, your dog will think you are the greatest.
- Remember, dogs are "warm in the hand."
- May you never walk alone.

# Medical Glossary

**Addison's Disease** Autoimmune disease associated with the adrenal glands

**Amyloidosis** Swollen joints early; later, renal failure

**Axonal dystrophy** Brain disease

**BAER test** Brainstem auditory evoked response, a test for deafness

**Cardiomyopathy** Damaged heart muscle

**CERF** Canine Eye Registry Foundation; certifies animals free of eye disease following ophthalmological exam

**CHD** Canine hip dysplasia. *See* HD

**Chondrodysplasia** Dwarfism

**CMO** Craniomandibular osteopathy; thickened lower jaw, causing pain

**Collie Eye Anomaly** Ectasia, an eye deformity ranging from minor to blindness

**Copper-associated hepatopathy** Selective accumulation of copper in liver, leading to liver failure

**Copper toxicosis** *See* Copper-associated hepatopathy

**Corneal dystrophy** White patches on eye surface

**Cystinuria** Condition that causes formation of bladder stones

**Degenerative Myelopathy** Muscle wasting and progressive ataxia (weakness)

**Dermoid cyst** Tubelike cyst into back; may communicate with spinal cord

**Distichiasis** Extra row of eyelashes that irritate cornea, causing tearing

**Ectropion** Hanging lower eyelids that accumulate irritants and create red, inflamed eyes

**Elongated soft palate and stenotic nares** Pinched nostrils and obstructed airway, causing snoring, gagging and exercise intolerance

**Entropion** Eyelids roll inward; hair rubs on cornea, causing tearing and scarring

**Fanconi's syndrome** Degeneration of renal tubes, leading to renal failure

**Gangliosidosis** Congenital lack of brain enzymes, leading to retardation, blindness and seizures within one year

**Geriatric spinal demyelinization** (myelopathy) Geriatric degeneration of the lower spinal cord

**Glomerulonephritis** Kidney disease

**Glycogen storage disease** GM-1; low blood sugar due to inherent liver enzyme deficiency, causing liver destruction

**HD** Hip dysplasia; progressive deformity of hip joints (see also CHD)

**Hemolytic anemia** Destruction of red blood cells by the body's own defenses; potentially fatal

**Histiocytosis** Complicated cancer attacking various organs

**HOD** Hypertrophic osteodystrophy; painful, swollen joints and bones; may leave bone deformities or even be fatal

**Inguinal hernia** Rupture in groin

**Legg-Perthes** (Legg-Calvé-Perthes) Degeneration of hip joint

**Lens luxation** Lens slips out of position, leading to glaucoma

**Lupus** Multiple-system autoimmune disease

**Lymphoma** Cancer of the blood

**Malabsorption** Inability to absorb digested food

**Microphthalmia** Very small eye globe

**MVD** Mitral valve defect; defect in valve between upper and lower heart chambers

**OCD** Osteochondritis dessicans; growth disorder of joints, resulting in pain and degeneration

**OFA** Orthopedic Foundation for Animals; a registry that certifies animals free of bone and joint disease following X-rays

**Open fontanel** When soft spot on skull does not close

**Optic nerve hypoplasia** Lack of development of nerve between eye and brain

**Pannus** Blood vessels bringing pigment over cornea; can lead to blindness

**Patellar luxation** When structures that hold kneecap in place are poor

**PDA** Patent ductus arteriosus—a heart birth defect

**Pemphigus** Autoimmune skin disease

**Perianal fistula** Open, draining tracts around anal orifice

**PKD** Pyruvate kinase deficiency; anemia due to premature red blood cell destruction

**PRA** Progressive retinal atrophy; retinal degeneration causing partial to total blindness

**Retinopathy** Abnormal formation of the retina, vision impairment

**Renal cortical hypoplasia** Degeneration of both kidneys

**SA** Sebaceous adenitis; degeneration of oil glands, causing loss of hair and constant skin infections

**SAS** Subaortic stenosis; congenitally narrowed heart valve

**Stenotic nares** *See* Elongated soft palate

**Torsion** Stomach rotates, causing bloat, shock and possible death

**Trichiasis** Eyelashes grow inward and irritate cornea

**vWD** (von Willebrand's Disease) A blood-clotting disorder

**Wobblers** (Cervical Vertebral Instability) Instability, weakness or paralysis of neck vertebrae

# Index